The Edgeryders guide to the future

A handbook
for policy makers and designers
of policy-oriented online communities

French edition:
Guide Edgeryders pour l'avenir
ISBN 978-92-871-7658-5

Acknowledgements

Compiling this report from the wealth of stories posted on the *Edgeryders* platform has been a pleasure and a challenge in equal measure. My aim has been to convey the breadth of Edgeryders' experiences in such a way as to draw together common concerns, framed in terms easily transposable to the policy domain. I extend thanks to the *Edgeryders* research team whose work has informed this report, the project team for their valued input, and, most of all, the Edgeryders for sharing their stories so vividly.

Rebecca Collins

Contributors: Alberto Cottica, Barbara Giovanni Di Bello, Ben Vickers, Dunja Potocnik, Gaia Marcus, Piotr Mikiewicz, Prudencia Gutiérrez Esteban, Magnus Eriksson, Rebecca Collins, Sladja Petkovic and Valentina Cuzzocrea

Creative direction for *The Edgeryders guide to the future:* Nadia El-Imam

Graphic design and illustrations: Malica Worms

Cover and layout: Documents and Publications Production Department (SPDP), Council of Europe

Council of Europe Publishing
F-67075 Strasbourg Cedex
http://book.coe.int

ISBN 978-92-871-7659-2
© Council of Europe, October 2013
Printed at the Council of Europe

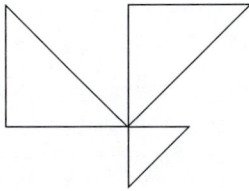

Contents

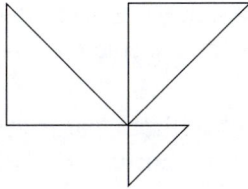

Foreword

Edgeryders[1] has been a unique experience for many of us working in public administration with responsibility for framing policies. This online platform, co-funded by the European Commission's Directorate-General for Employment, Social Affairs & Inclusion and by the Council of Europe, had a specific aim: to understand, via an innovative approach which deliberately sought not to impose any institutional forms of dialogue, the difficulties faced by young Europeans and the solutions they come up with, based on their experiences of the transition towards an independent life in a rapidly changing, increasingly insecure environment.

The platform was designed to freely encourage horizontal interaction and exchanges. Nevertheless, at a time when the speed of communication means that opinions are expressed in just a few sentences – often using shortcuts that are understandable only to the initiated – *Edgeryders* asked the young participants to focus their voluntary participation on six themes or "campaigns": Making a Living; We, the People; Living Together; Caring for Commons; Learning; and Resilience.[2] They were asked to produce "mission reports" or comments in response to open questions which were always formulated in co-operation, both within the Council of Europe and with the participants themselves.

---

1. Throughout this guide, the term "Edgeryder(s)" will refer to project participants while the italicised *"Edgeryders"* will refer to the project and the online platform.
2. Resilience can generally be understood as the capacity of humans to come out of an extreme shock, damage and trauma and adapt to new living conditions.

Why did the Council of Europe create this prototype of an interactive dialogue with young citizens? Some reasons included:

– encouraging institutions to take a fresh look at those they serve, and in particular giving voice to the valuable contribution that citizens can make;

– obtaining a better idea of the extent of insecurity in society. Exclusion, growing vulnerability and the lack of prospects are no longer solely the lot of those without qualifications. Instability is becoming a way of life for many, so there has to be a new political response;

– drawing attention to the political interpretation of statistics, particularly where they flag up a problem in society. For example, the statistics on NEETs (Not in Employment, Education or Training) place a large proportion of young people and their potential in a black hole. A different approach that prioritises this human potential and the solutions young people come up with to deal with emerging insecurity can influence policy choices.

What has the Council of Europe learned? Amongst other things, that:

– legitimacy and institutional commitment can facilitate constructive dialogue;

– it is possible to reconcile citizens and institutions if there is mutual trust and if each can learn from the other;

– by considering the experiences and creativity of citizens to be knowledge tools, public policies can make a greater impact and bring about change;

– it is possible to work with vulnerable groups without necessarily stigmatising them and that – contrary to the widespread perception of "problem groups" – these sections of the community have interests in and opinions on a wide range of societal issues;

– horizontal relationships (peer-to-peer, sharing, commons) and networked interaction can provide fresh meaning and new solutions in order to satisfy needs, without any additional pressure on existing resources;

– learning is not necessarily top-down;

– creativity is fundamental to policy design and a true knowledge tool to discover the full potential, rather than just the limits, of citizens and their situations;

– in order to build the future, it is essential to co-operate with those whose future it will be.

There are also many questions raised by this type of online tool.

Responding to citizens' expectations often presents public authorities with a real challenge. It is not merely a question of addressing existing inertia, but of establishing a balance between what authorities and elected representatives can do and what they can – in contrast – facilitate. In a spirit of co-operation, authorities and elected representatives can promote the sharing of responsibilities, ideas, goods and values so as to involve society in horizontal, inclusive, solidarity-based and social cohesion-oriented approaches.

Over and above the challenges of how to structure a response to the question of citizen participation, an interactive tool requires a good measure of internal institutional readiness to act in terms of follow-up and response, and above all a willingness to give fresh political meaning to dialogue. This presupposes giving value to solutions that emerge from interactions with citizens.

There are also questions concerning the users of online tools. Despite growing Internet access in Europe, the chances of interacting with citizens will depend on their level of interest in public affairs. It is not easy to reach vulnerable groups who feel they have no influence. In order to raise interest and sustain dialogue in the long term, online interaction must be followed up by concrete measures and by a demonstration of the legitimacy of citizen action for fostering inclusion.

These thoughts would not be complete without some words of thanks. The design and development of the prototype are thanks to the intelligence and passion of Alberto Cottica and Nadia El-Imam. Noemi Salantiu, Lyne Robichaud, Chara Oikonomidou and Vinay Gupta played their role as engagement managers. Rebecca Collins, Valentina Cuzzocrea, Barbara Giovanna Bello, Dunja Potocnik, Sladjana Petkovic, Magnus Eriksson, Piotr Mikiewicz and Prudencia Gutiérrez Esteban, by using their research skills and applying ethnographical analysis to the data, gave meaning to the mission reports and participants' comments. They helped us understand their experiences while retaining the power of the individual messages. Ivan Vaghi and Paolo Mainardi contributed with their professional competences to the technical development of the platform.

Many other participants in what is now known as the *"Edgeryders* community" contributed their time, thoughts and passion to this work. Among Council of Europe staff, Malcolm Cox has put in particular effort.

I should also like to thank the Council of Europe's Committee for Social Cohesion, whose members have lent their support to the process and have found in *Edgeryders* a means of generating hope and renewal.

This guide is – like the platform itself – the result of co-ordinated but free expression. We have not sought to smooth out any rough edges in the text, for without rough edges, humankind cannot provide the footholds its individual members need to develop.

We hope that we have contributed to the debate on the purpose of policies to facilitate transition and inclusion in response to growing insecurity. Above all, we hope we have been able to alert people to the urgent need for political and societal renewal in order to avoid sacrificing the knowledge and skills of the younger generations. For without them, our European society will be unable to recover the ability to contemplate its future.

Gilda Farrell
Head of Division
Social Cohesion, Research and Early Warning Division
Council of Europe

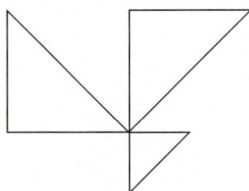

Executive summary

As a result of complex, interlinked socio-economic challenges, young people in Europe today are in a precarious position. Issues of education, employment, housing, personal well-being and political participation all have a part to play in this precariousness. The sheer number and scale of the problems young people are facing mean that many feel paralysed by insecurity, frustrated both by the lack of recognition of their plight and the lack of institutional support. It is in this context that the *Edgeryders* project was devised as a means to deepening understanding of the specific challenges young Europeans are facing in their attempts to successfully navigate the transition to an independent and active life. *Egderyders* also serves as a live account for some of the innovative and creative ways youth address those challenges. The project is fundamentally premised on the construction of youth as part of the solution, rather than an intrinsic social problem.

The data generated by the project was used to (a) offer an insight into the participants' everyday lives and the challenges faced in the course of their transitions; and (b) provide a channel of direct communication with policy makers in terms of support structures and mechanisms. This report presents a range of Edgeryders' experiences, expressed in the context of the project as a means to articulating the need for action in specific policy domains. It focuses both on the most important policy themes (such as education, employment and housing) and on the ways in which policy is made and delivered in practice. It is hoped that the points raised will inform the development of youth-focused policies that are not only well targeted and responsive to current challenges, but also characterised by methods of delivery in which citizens are actively involved as opposed to being imposed upon.

One of the main learning points that came out of the interaction among members of the *Edgeryders* platform is that they possess an impressive wealth of knowledge, talent and commitment to make a living, without compromising their lifestyles. They also have the ability to share and collaborate on their own terms by doing things that matter for a wider audience, rather than for a particular employer. They are increasingly concerned, however, about issues such as exploitation for cheap labour and marginalisation, either for non-compliance with existing state programmes or for finding solutions in alternative ways. Additionally, the transition from adolescence to adulthood is a highly fragmented process that does not have a clear end point and does not just concern youth in their 20s. Against this backdrop, the increasing devaluation and obsolescence of higher education diplomas and qualifications affect the way individuals configure their personal expectations. In fact, this leaves room for youth to acquire much broader skill sets through diverse forms of learning in both physical and virtual settings.

Finally, the *Edgeryders* project has shown that technological changes can bring citizens closer to the complex workings of politics. Using the virtual world as a new channel, youth capitalises on the open space for manoeuvre and interaction and, rather than turning away, it reinvents its relationship with the establishment. Thus, networks like *Edgeryders* are becoming a complement to the role of the family in terms of the alliances or care and support that they can provide, especially during times when state safety nets are weakened or absent.

Drawing directly on Edgeryders' contributions, the report outlines four areas in which they have described a particular mismatch between current policies and young people's actual needs and lived experiences:

— there are conflicting ideas about what constitutes value in the realms of work, education and community. Edgeryders argue the need for new concepts of value to accommodate more diverse forms of productivity, more collaborative forms of learning, and shared access to common resources;

— positive change can be brought about swiftly and efficiently by aggregating effort and sharing existing knowledge. Edgeryders suggest that policy mechanisms based on open data can empower communities to act in ways that fulfil their own needs more efficiently and with greater agility than that which can be achieved by institutions;

— there is a mutual lack of trust between young citizens and institutions. Edgeryders need institutions to be allies, rather than enforcers of poorly targeted policies. They want institutional commitment to viewing the lived impacts of policies on the ground, and bringing those findings into policy making.

—   there is a pressing need for new cultural norms which accommodate young people's transitions in an increasingly difficult socio-economic climate. A key part of this should be the development of a new language to describe young people's transitions, the kinds of lives and futures they are seeking and the terms on which they want their contributions to be valued.

In a "Call to action" addressed directly to policy institutions, the report underlines the need for new policies which respond quickly and fully to these imperatives. Edgeryders stress the importance of policy-making processes which make use of young people's lived experiences, and they call for policy makers to engage with these personally by engaging with young people in their own spaces (both real and virtual). Edgeryders need institutions to embrace what they describe as "Policy 2.0" and they are demonstrably willing to play their part in shaping innovative processes of citizen–institution collaboration.

The report concludes by reiterating the need for a pluralistic approach to policies concerned with youth in order to respond dynamically to the increasingly complex, variable and protracted nature of transition to independent adulthood. Some reflections are included on the ways in which *Edgeryders*, as a research project, has brought these important points to light, and thus can be viewed as a successful model on which future collaborative exercises might be modelled.

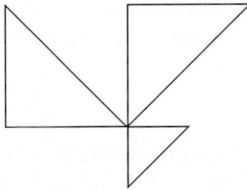

How to use this guide

This handbook for policy makers is an overview of the *Edgeryders* project, an open and distributed think tank of young Europeans that works through an interactive online platform. Developed by the Social Cohesion Research and Early Warning Division at the Council of Europe, *Edgeryders* was tasked with looking at the transition from youth to independent, active life, employing a holistic perspective. The project encompasses an arc of 13 months at the time of writing (September 2011 to September 2012). An unusual project that embraced the Internet as the main meeting place and locus of co-ordination for all its activities, *Edgeryders* had to innovate its administrative modus operandi at every step just to stay viable. This document tries to summarise the operational knowledge gathered along the way as well as the implications for members of the policy community.

The handbook is divided into two sections. The first section, "On being Edgeryders", presents the research results from the ethnographic analysis of the data collected. It gives the reader an insight into why the young people who have become Edgeryders matter, and what their stories reveal about the current disconnect between their ambitions for an active, independent life and the socio-political arena in which they are attempting to make these a reality. Through the numbers of participants engaged over the year, the *Edgeryders* project has generated a wealth of data, reaching a breadth and depth that most other forms of policy research have, to date, rarely sought to achieve.

The second section, "Transitioning into the future", puts forward proposals for action as suggested by project participants, the team of policy researchers and experts charged with devising the policy recommendations as well as the Social Cohesion Research and Early Warning Division of the Council of Europe.

Appendix A presents the political background to the *Edgeryders* project, the policy-led reasons as to why a risk has been taken on this unusual approach, as well as a guide to how the project was built for those who wish to replicate this methodology. Its purpose is to serve as a guide for managers of future policy-oriented online communities.

Appendix B is a letter from the *Edgeryders* community about possible funding and support mechanisms that the contributors wanted to share with funders (charities, governments, companies, development agencies, and so on).

While the first iteration of the project is wrapping up, *Edgeryders* is a generative project both for institutions and for the individual citizens who engage in it. It has been invited to and continues to feed into other institutional projects. The *Edgeryders* methodology for crowdsourcing knowledge has been commissioned to contribute to the Parliamentary Assembly of the Council of Europe report on addressing suicide and self-harm prevention amongst young people in Europe,[3] and has been picked up in a new joint project between the European Commission and the Council of Europe for combating poverty, exclusion and precarisation. For individual community members, *Edgeryders* as an initiative has had a far more significant impact than playing a role in policy research; it has already started to provide support for this community on a peer-to-peer basis. This is supported by the high level of visibility and attention the project enjoys in different fora: project team members have been invited to present the project methodology and findings at Learning Without Frontiers,[4] TEDxLiege,[5] TedxBologna,[6] Social Media Week Berlin,[7] the Social Capital World Forum[8] and so on. Members of the *Edgeryders* community independently organised an event that took place in Brussels in December 2012, where people from all over Europe participated on a voluntary basis, travelling at their own expense.

---

3. "Learning to live", a collaboratively produced report on suicide and self-harm prevention amongst young people in Europe, available at http://scribd.com/doc/104169463/Edgeryders-Community-Paper-Learning-To-Live, accessed 18 July 2013.
4. "How do governments learn to do new things?", Nadia El-Imam at Learning Without Frontiers, available at http://lwf12.sched.org/directory/speakers/#.UKvCtc3tGZl, accessed 18 July 2013.
5. "The Edgeryders Guide to New Europe", Nadia El-Imam at TEDxULg, available at http://youtu.be/I5ffVJRLAdk, accessed 18 July 2013.
6. "Designing collective intelligence – Alberto Cottica at TEDxBologna", available at http://youtu.be/KKrM2c-ww_k, accessed 18 July 2013.
7. "The rise of the citizen expert", Alberto Cottica and Nadia El-Imam at Social Media Week Berlin, available at http://socialmediaweek.org/blog/event/the-rise-of-the-citizen-expert/#.UKvDUM3tGZl, accessed 18 July 2013.
8. "Rise of the citizen expert", Nadia El-Imam at the Social Capital World Forum 2012 Sweden, available at http://scwf12.files.wordpress.com/2012/11/scwf12-gothenburg-flyer-v121114.pdf, accessed 18 July 2013.

In this document we have used many quotations from Edgeryders' conversations to render the lively participatory atmosphere of the online platform and the physical meetings. These quotations are attributed to aliases used by participants on the online *Edgeryders* platform for privacy. Where full names have been used it is because participants chose them as their online monikers. In addition to the authors' own material, materials posted on the *Edgeryders* platform are used under a Creative Commons license.

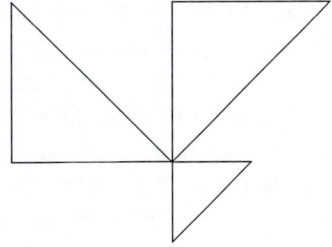

I. On being Edgeryders

A picture of young Europeans navigating the transition to an independent life
Rebecca Collins and Valentina Cuzzocrea[9]

Introduction

Edgeryders was launched in October 2011 as a "social game" and "peer-to-peer learning environment" with three main aims. The first of these has been to provide information, encouragement and support to a generation of young Europeans who are striving to build futures based on meaningful work and political participation in the most challenging socio-economic climate in several decades. The second aim has been to explore the stories of project participants in order to better understand the specific challenges they feel they face, as well as their goals and aspirations, and the resources they draw on to support their pursuit of a satisfying and successful life. The third and overriding aim has been to use the information generated by the "think tank" approach adopted by this project to inform policy initiatives around young people's transitions to adulthood.

---

9. This section is the result of a collaboration between the two authors, who share the views expressed here. The content under the headings "Risks", "Resources" and "Scale" were drafted by Rebecca Collins (University College London), and the content under "The many layers of the *Edgeryders* platform", "Values and motivations" and "Responses" by Valentina Cuzzocrea (University of Kent). Both authors contributed equally to "Introduction" and "Conclusions".

Although it is increasingly acknowledged that the notion of transition is applicable throughout the life course (Worth 2009), this project is concerned specifically with youth transitions. The literature identifies five thresholds which have to be navigated on the path to full adulthood: completion of education; attaining a relatively stable working position; leaving the family of origin; forming a relationship; and parenthood. This concept of transition has a strong regulatory framework in the sense that it is characterised by specific expectations about what should be achieved and in what time frame. However, since the passages to full adulthood are becoming more fragmented, reversible and generally delayed (Cavalli and Galland 1996; Miles 2000), this framework has become increasingly problematic. As a result, a growing body of research around youth studies has emerged and is devoted to the exploration of the issues specific to today's youth (Walther 2006; Arnett 2007; Côté 2009; Wyn 2004; White and Wyn 2008; Leccardi and Ruspini 2006), sometimes called the "Y generation"[10] to distinguish it from previous generations of youth, each of which has its own characteristics. In this report, we present an analysis of Edgeryders' experiences when navigating these transitions, as expressed through mission reports on the online platform and in response to the invitation to "get help, inspire others, make sense of it all".

First, it is important to be clear who the Edgeryders are. Since this is a European-funded project[11] it is unsurprising that the vast majority of participants are based within Europe. Edgeryders have been most commonly based in France, Italy or the UK, which is likely a reflection of the networks employed to generate participation in the project.[12] In terms of the numbers of participants, these three countries are followed by the US, Spain, Germany, Sweden, Canada, Belgium and Romania. Over 900 people have registered as users with the platform, with almost 200 of these being regular contributors. The ratio of men to women participating is approximately 2:1. Edgeryders are not asked to divulge their age in order to participate so an accurate statement about typical age is not possible. However, based on the life events commonly discussed in mission reports, it is clear that the majority of participants are between the ages of 20 and 30, although there are some regular contributors in their 40s and 50s. A more detailed analysis of the characteristics of the network's

---

10. For a discussion of the Y generation at work, see Kelan 2009.

11. *Edgeryders* is funded by the European Commission and the Council of Europe. The implementation of the project is the responsibility of the Social Cohesion, Research and Early Warning Division of the Council of Europe, and falls within a Social Cohesion Joint Programme titled Europe of Welfare for All: Facilitating Youth Transition to Active Life by Reinforcing Shared Social Responsibilities.

12. It should be noted, however, that the country in which an Edgeryder was based at the time of participation did not necessarily correspond with his or her nationality. Many Edgeryders were extremely mobile and travelled within and beyond Europe a great deal.

participants has been produced by Gaia Marcus and Ben Vickers (2012) in the form of a network analysis.[13]

As with age, stating one's level of education has not been a prerequisite for participation, although given the nature of the *Edgeryders* project, this has often been incorporated into mission reports. As such, it is possible to describe Edgeryders' levels of education in general terms. A significant majority are university educated, with many holding postgraduate qualifications. Perhaps more important than formal qualifications, however, is the fact that many participants engage in forms of learning or education via online services/networks that demonstrate their high intellectual abilities. This in turn gives an indication of the types of young people who have engaged with the *Edgeryders* project – highly literate in information and communications technology (ICT), knowledge hungry, and keen to contribute to knowledge as well as receive it. However, and very much in line with other studies on the theme of education-to-work transitions (Bynner and Parsons 2002; Heinz 2002; Lehmann 2004; Pinquart et al. 2003), this high level of education does not correspond to economic security. Edgeryders' accounts often problematise such difficulties, thus framing the platform as a dynamic space within which possible solutions to this complex issue can be discussed.

In this publication we present the key findings of the *Edgeryders* project, based on an analysis of the textual material generated through the online platform. New media have become a rich methodological resource for social scientists over the last two decades (Turkle 1995), and in particular they have helped to open up new ways of researching and interpreting human conduct and identity issues. More recently, researchers have begun to propose specific forms of online ethnography which acknowledge and aim to address the challenges faced by researchers in these contexts (Beneito-Montagut 2011; Hookway 2008; Jones 1999). This special attention is justified by the importance of inclusive participation (Borg et al. 2012), which, in the case of *Edgeryders*, is particularly relevant given the difficulties in engaging youth in consultation (Dentith et al. 2012). We have dealt with the richness of the data created by *Edgeryders* by using WEFT QDA, a free qualitative data analysis software package. All of the data produced through the platform up to the Living on the Edge conference in mid-June 2012 has been coded,[14] although we also incorporate in the present discussion comments which appeared

---

13. See http://edgeryders.ppa.coe.int/help-build-june-conference/mission_case/edgeryders-social-network-analysis-fullreport, accessed 18 July 2013.

14. This date is in accordance with the original project plan. It must be remembered that *Edgeryders* is a prototype; as such, it was difficult to anticipate the quantity and quality of data that would emerge over the course of the project, including the meetings in Strasbourg. Overall, there has been a high number of very good quality reports and it is a testament to the success of the project that mission reports were still being created more than a month after the Living on the Edge conference (LOTE).

after this date, as well as comments made during the two *Edgeryders* conferences (15-16 March and 14-15 June 2012). The coded texts will be shared online to allow the community to conduct their own searches based on our codes (that is, keywords or tags identified with concepts), as well as allowing other researchers to consult, further edit and use them for subsequent projects. Having taken a grounded approach in which the direction of analysis is led by the content of the data (Glaser and Strauss 1967; Charmaz 2006), the themes presented here represent the dominant issues of concern to participants, and some of their most common responses.

The main body of the report is structured around what we have identified as the six core facets of Edgeryders' transitions. First, we analyse the various "layers" of the interaction process that *Edgeryders* puts forward. Second, as a means of framing the analytical themes we employ through Edgeryders' own perspectives, we outline the commonly held values and motivations that underpin the ways in which participants engage with society. Third, we present four key risks that Edgeryders face in the course of their transitions. Fourth, we discuss the range of resources that they draw on in their attempts to manage these risks and respond with positive action. Here we also consider what limits these resources and how institutions might be able to provide valuable support. Fifth, we present some of the ways in which Edgeryders make use of their resources to respond to the risks they face. Focusing on the ways in which they work in pursuit of an active and meaningful life for themselves and their communities, our aim here is to illustrate Edgeryders' ability to be creative, dynamic and innovative in the context of sporadic external support. The sixth theme concerns the scale(s) at which Edgeryders act, specifically the relationship between global socio-economic challenges and local action, mediated by global technology networks. We conclude with a discussion of the ways in which Edgeryders' actions can be interpreted as building both personal and collective (community) resilience.

1. The multiple layers of the *Edgeryders* platform

To any reader of Edgeryders' posts, the contents of their discussions appear rich, informed, and, above all, genuine. *Edgeryders* has configured itself as an expressive tool for its participants, one which allows – even encourages – respectful communication and exchanges. However, this is only the surface appearance of a complex machine made up of several layers, each of which has its own meanings and function (Figure 1). Since this project is framed as an exercise in democratic public participation, it is important to acknowledge that the open and collaborative space of *Edgeryders* as a platform has worked to generate conceptual understandings of contemporary youth transitions capable of directly and usefully informing youth policies beyond the thematic analyses and discussions presented by the research team.

Figure 1: The layers of interaction within the *Edgeryders* platform (arrows show the feedback flows of information)

It should be noted that Edgeryders' stories are often extremely detailed and tell us a lot about the socio-economic contexts in which they are working through their transitions to independent adult life. As a result, the platform constitutes more than a site where interactions among peers are played out around specific discussion foci. It is also a documentary source offering a window into the real-life settings in which young people's lives – with their challenges and innovative solutions – are played out. In the analysis presented here our aim has been to synthesise commonalities within the data while also creating space to render individual stories visible. We feel it is also important to acknowledge the richness of the data gathered through this project; with the community's permission much further productive use could be made of it.

2. Values and motivations

Edgeryders is an experiment that was created in and resulted from a persistently difficult economic climate across Europe. Notably, youth are being affected more profoundly in this crisis than other groups. In particular, youth unemployment rates have reached dramatic levels, with several countries reaching 30% and some others, such as Greece and Spain, in excess of 50%.[15] At least in countries where education is free or relatively cheap, some young people presently excluded from the labour market have entered into prolonged periods of education.

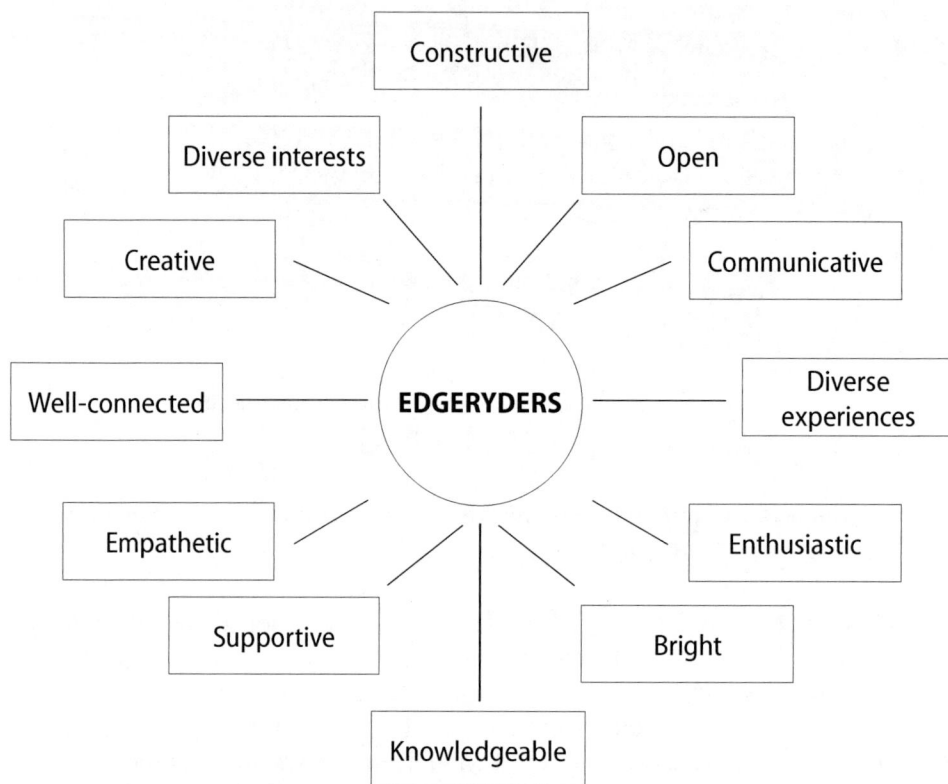

```
                        Constructive

        Diverse interests              Open

    Creative                              Communicative

Well-connected        EDGERYDERS         Diverse
                                         experiences

    Empathetic                            Enthusiastic

        Supportive                     Bright

                      Knowledgeable
```

Figure 2: Traits shared by *Edgeryders* participants

While it cannot be said that furthering one's education is, in itself, a mistake, there are situations where this can exacerbate the problems of employment, as education also nurtures personal and professional aspirations which are increasingly difficult to fulfil, at least following traditional pathways. Of course, this catch-22 situation assumes slightly different contours in relation to specific countries, and, more generally, to the models of welfare which govern socio-political areas in Europe.[16] The generalised lack of employment opportunities is therefore to be seen not only as an economic problem,

15. Available at www.oecd-ilibrary.org/employment/youth-unemployment-rate_20752342-table2, accessed 18 July 2013.
16. Traditionally, these are divided following Esping-Andersen's categorisation (1990, 1999).

but also as a socio-cultural problem bound up with established generational relations (and associated social expectations and norms), with youth today perhaps expected to achieve less (in terms of money, security, status and so on) than their parents' generation, despite having studied longer. Furthermore, there was a strong sense across the *Edgeryders* platform that business and government have remained wedded to the status quo in terms of the forms of employment promoted – both institutions are perceived as being nervous about supporting forms of work that they see as "too innovative". One Edgeryder, Tiago, expressed this in his presentation at the March 2012 mini-conference when he suggested that young job seekers are being told by potential employers, "I am sorry, you are too ahead of your time."[17]

In this chapter, we seek to identify the values and motivations that drive young people's actions in the context of such pervasive socio-economic difficulties. This allows us to create a broad framework within which a subsequent discussion of Edgeryders' responses to these difficulties can be situated. The core characteristics shared by participants are presented in Figure 2. First, it is clear that Edgeryders strive to be part of a movement for change larger than their individual efforts. They are committed to using their skills and knowledge to address economic, political, social and environmental realities, and are doing so in ways that draw on their own diverse career experiences in order to offer support for others. Many Edgeryders' paths are characterised by frequent change, uncertainty and instability but these are associated with particularly high levels of personal satisfaction as a result of bringing a diverse skills set to bear on varied projects. There also seems to be a shared aspiration amongst Edgeryders to feel more alive or more human as individuals, in large part in response to a general working culture perceived as conformist and dehumanising. But the desire of Edgeryders to be part of a "community" of change is not only about creating a context to which they want to contribute; it seems equally to be about a personal quest for self-efficacy and validation – in many ways a personal journey embedded within a shared one – for which individuals are frequently prepared to make material sacrifices. Whether the focus is urban farming or knowledge sharing, Edgeryders' projects are often directly or indirectly linked to the production of new modes of living and working, such as Lucyanna's[18] and Bridget McKenzie's[19] posts on a form of family life that prioritises

17. Available at www.scribd.com/doc/85580648/Edgeryders-Making-a-Living-by-Making-a-Difference, accessed 18 July 2013.
18. Lucyanna, "Spotlight: meet my family!: family life – a myth", available at http:// edgeryders.wikispiral. org/spotlight-meet-my-family/mission_case/family-life-myth, accessed 18 July 2013.
19. Bridget McKenzie, "Spotlight: meet my family!: creative home-based living", available at http://edgeryders.ppa.coe.int/spotlight-meet-my-family/mission_case/creative-home-based-living, accessed 18 July 2013.

human relationships over work demands, Edwin's[20] co-operative living-working space, and Carlien Roodink's musings on why we have ceased to think that an alternative model to the employment society can actually work.[21] As such, Edgeryders are individuals who strive to understand existing systems and work out solutions as to how they can be improved, made more egalitarian or more accessible, in ways that better respond to human needs. Ultimately, we draw attention to three key values: integrity, passion and autonomy.

Integrity

Integrity not only encapsulates the wider set of values many Edgeryders appear to hold, it is seen as foundational to individual prosperity. A key question during the "Making a living" session at the Living on the Edge (LOTE) conference was "How does this [form of work you are inventing] create value?" One Edgeryder, elf Pavlik, has lived for more than three years strictly moneyless and stateless:

> [he] gets the things he needs through sharing. He works on projects without asking for anything in return, supporting causes he cares about. Similarly when people support him with food and shelter, he hitchhikes to travel from place to place, it happens just because people want to support him and what he does. No money is exchanged.[22]

Pavlik refuses citizenship and holds no passport. Another Edgeryder, Jean Russell, expressed the extent to which focus and self-awareness are fundamental to her personal sense of integrity in her "Share your ryde" mission report:

> I had felt like everything I had been doing was intentional and aiming toward a good life, but my perspective had been narrow. I went through a massive overhaul toward a much deeper level of integrity. And along with it suffered a great deal of guilt. [...] The guilt was accompanied by a lot of gratitude, so I never would have spoken of it as guilt at the time. I was grateful for what life had given me. But underneath that was a guilt over the privilege I felt.[23]

---

20. Edwin, "Mine becomes ours: a few of us. Living together (somewhere) and changing things?: the (un) Monastery", available at http://edgeryders.ppa.coe.int/mine-becomes-ours/mission_case/few-us-living-together-somewhere-and-changing-things-unmonastery, accessed 18 July 2013.
21. Carlien Roodink, "The quest for paid work: we should organize our society around something else than employment", available at http://edgeryders.ppa.coe.int/quest-paid-work/mission_case/we-should-organize-our-society-around-something-else-employment, accessed 18 July 2013.
22. Cataspanglish has posted a video interview with elf Pavlik as a mission report, "The quest for paid work: (making a) living on the edge – elf Pavlik", available at http://edgeryders.ppa.coe.int/quest-paid-work/mission_case/making-living-edge-elf-pavlik, accessed 22 July 2013.
23. Jean Russell, "Share your ryde: transparency and living well", available at http:// edgeryders.ppa.coe.int/share-your-ryde/mission_case/transparency-and-living-well, accessed 22 July 2013.

Equally revealing are the stories of Alessia Zabatino, who in the mission report "Addiopizzo. Aware consumers against the Mafia system"[24] talks about a volunteer association which opposes the mafia system in Sicily, and Noemi Salantiu, discussing her career aspirations:

> I never thought of salary as a reward for my work because I just had other priority indicators to measure my satisfaction with work – not revenues, but quality. For me, an indicator of success in making a living so far has been knowledge and personal growth no matter what I would do. What's very important is to be able to do my work well, really well, and gain some recognition.[25]

Passion

Passion is widely evident in the narratives of Edgeryders' paths, especially in the mission brief "Share your ryde". It is a primary motivating force, not only in terms of giving direction and maximising opportunities to find meaningful work, but also as being worth much more than money. Passion is central to sustaining openness within one's own lifestyle, as Noemi suggests: "Even when you don't have a career plan, things may turn out well just because at any given time you're where you want to be and doing what you love."[26] The legitimisation of following one's passion implies diversification and the acceptance of diverging paths as a normal part of one's personal growth. In "My work is my hobby!" Ioana Traistă states what is important for her:

> Contributing to social change is the only way that I can feel my personal and professional life will have a purpose. Communications for NGOs, NGO organizational capacity building, community engagement, social entrepreneurship – these are the things that bring joy in my life. I definitely know that along the way, I will discover other things that will add up to these ones, but I know for sure that we cannot afford ourselves the compromise not to do what we are meant for.[27]

---

24. Alessia Zabatino, "Reactivating democratic institutions: Addiopizzo. Aware consumers against the Mafia system", available at http://edgeryders.ppa.coe.int/reactivating-democratic-institutions/mission_case/addiopizzo-aware-consumers-against-mafia-system, accessed 22 July 2013.
25. Noemi Salantiu, "The quest for paid work: I look for recognition in my work", available at http://edgeryders.ppa.coe.int/quest-paid-work/mission_case/i-look-recognition-my-work, accessed 22 July 2013.
26. Noemi Salantiu, in a comment on higiacomo's mission report, "The quest for paid work: passion->volunteer->job->... passion again?", available at http://edgeryders.ppa.coe.int/quest-paid-work/mission_case/passion-volunteer-job-passion-again, accessed 22 July 2013.
27. Ioana Traistă, "Share your ryde: my work is my hobby!", available at http://edgeryders.ppa.coe.int/share-your-ryde/mission_case/my-work-my-hobby, accessed 22 July 2013.

DarioMazzella is equally outspoken about his motivations for engaging in international civil and political action:

> Experiences like these can empower the youth, by giving us the chance to shape the future we want and to influence the civil society. It's not about age or political parties, it's about to be passionate and responsible!!![28]

Luna Islands Tsukino comments on Irene Fazio's mission report "To be an innovator you must be volcanic!", where Irene talks about a business plan competition called Vulcanica-Mente, which supports bright ideas for start-ups:

> I really like the idea of Vulcanica-Mente!! I think it's great in such difficult time periods to give hope and support for people to build their own ventures! I'm working at Hub Vienna and I see daily this hope on their faces when they enter the place and this gives me so much enthusiasm and power to move on![29]

Autonomy

Autonomy was the third key motivation underpinning Edgeryders' stories. Despite systemic difficulties, many Edgeryders are eager to achieve on their own terms without being dependent on external forces, suggesting that they possess real confidence in both themselves and their plans. As Pete Ashton argues:

> it's about taking control and responsibility for your activities and presence and not complaining that the system doesn't let you do that – forget the system, I'll make my own way.[30]

However, it is important to emphasise that this autonomy, rather than being self-centred or short-sighted, takes a communitarian and forward-looking perspective. This is not a contradiction in terms. Autonomy here is about more than just an individualised transition; it is a personal journey embedded within a shared one. Whilst it is partly a personal quest for self-efficacy and validation, it is also about being part of a "community" of change – about creating a context to which Edgeryders want to contribute. In this sense, the desire for autonomy is an ethical response because it is developed

---

28. DarioMazzella, "Share your ryde: G8 & G20 youth summits: a best practice to share because the time for youth involvement is now!", available at http://edgeryders.wikispiral.org/share-your-ryde/mission_case/g8-g20-youth-summits-best-practice-share-because-time-youth-involvement, accessed 22 July 2013.
29. Luna Islands Tsukino commenting on Irene Fazio's mission report, "Spotlight: social innovation: to be an innovator you must be volcanic!", available at http://edgeryders.ppa.coe.int/spotlight-social-innovation/mission_case/be-innovator-you-must-be-volcanic, accessed 22 July 2013.
30. Cataspanglish has posted an interview with Pete Ashton as a mission report, "The quest for paid work: (making a) living on the edge – Pete Ashton", available at http://edgeryders.wikispiral.org/quest-paid-work/mission_case/making-living-edge, accessed 22 July 2013.

in the name of the common good. It is an autonomy that does not depend on others, but is encapsulated in collaboration with others, as the discussions on the many forms of co-working, co-housing and other forms of sharing demonstrate. In this way, one's own path is invested with collective value, and, as a result, what Edgeryders both express and seek might best be described as "collective autonomy" – the freedom to share and collaborate on their own terms. Notably, the diffusion of the Internet and the possibilities to interact through it has meant that the flourishing of autonomy is increasingly facilitated, as many examples in the Caring for Commons campaign reveal. Edgeryder Said Hamideh's post and the community's comments on crowdsourcing offer a prime example.[31]

The centrality of integrity, passion and autonomy to Edgeryders' transitions are eloquently summarised by Alberto Masetti-Zannini:

> In conclusion: what do I look for in a job? Today – having gone through the rabbit hole and come out the other way – I look for meaning and purpose. I only want to do things that fit into a bigger scheme, and that make sense for our future. I want to do things that are not morally dubious. I look at the people I will be working with: I do not want to work with people I don't respect and value.[32]

Examples such as those discussed here imply a positive attitude towards change and the willingness and sincere desire to shape the world in a way that makes it more equal and prosperous for everybody. However, Edgeryders' attempts to implement this do not come without difficulties.

3. Risks

Edgeryders reported encountering a number of risks in the course of their transitions. These varied in nature, from the ways in which young people are characterised by institutions as cheap labour or as a threat to law and order, to the effects of failing to conform to a variety of widely held social norms.

One of the most commonly shared anxieties was fear of exploitation. There were two specific areas of concern. First was the sense of obligation attached to taking on low-value, low-paid work in order to either gain work experience or simply make enough money to pay for rent, bills and food. Sometimes low-grade work was a means of

---

31. Said Hamideh, "Spotlight: the internet as a common resource: towards a crowdsourced problem-solving platform that promotes citizen action and participation within politically fragmented nation-states", available at http://edgeryders.ppa.coe.int/spotlight-internet-common-resource/mission_case/towards-crowdsourced-problem-solving-platform-promot, accessed 22 July 2013.
32. Alberto Masetti-Zannini, "The quest for paid work: like Alice in Wonderland", available at http:// edgeryders.ppa.coe.int/quest-paid-work/mission_case/alice-wonderland, accessed 22 July 2013.

making enough money to live while more meaningful work was pursued simultaneously for no money. For most Edgeryders it has simply not been possible to gain experience or develop their own projects without financial support. The second area of concern addressed the practice of working for free. While volunteering was described in resoundingly positive terms as an experience where much more was learned than skills for a particular form of employment (for example self-awareness and sensitivity to particular social issues), unpaid internships were widely criticised for being exploitative and discriminatory. As IdilM said:

> I honestly do not understand how they expect young people just coming out of education (with huge debts) to be able to work full time for free, pay for their flights, accommodation and daily sustenance. These organizations either assume that everyone is rich or they are turning a blind eye to the plight of the disadvantaged and financially less well-off in society, thereby entrenching social inequalities.[33]

While it was agreed that internships generally constitute a valuable opportunity for skills development and networking, the lack of financial recompense was pricing large proportions of young people out of this opportunity. Moreover, anxiety about acquiring the broadest range of experience in order to increase future employability perpetuates back-to-back interning through which institutions are able to take advantage of young people's precariousness.

For a smaller group of Edgeryders, criminalisation was a concern. For some this involved being cast as "work-avoiders", through the removal of state welfare support from those unwilling to reduce their work with community or social enterprise projects in order to comply with state employment programmes. More common, however, was anxiety about the criminalisation of the appropriation of public resources by young people, particularly buildings and other public spaces, which several Edgeryders use for community benefit.

The third risk to which many Edgeryders were sensitive was marginalisation. They were anxious about the apparent lack of support for those unwilling to conform to existing models of employment or comply with state programmes. In other words, Edgeryders feel distanced from peers and communities as a result of their commitment to a different form of transition and working life. Several expressed significant worry about choices they had made about their working lives in the past, and it was an equally large source of concern for those facing similar decisions in the near future. In one sense this is a broad socio-cultural issue but it is one that has its roots in resistance to alternative

---

33. IdilM, "The quest for paid work: unpaid internships are discriminatory and should be ended.", available at http://edgeryders.ppa.coe.int/quest-paid-work/mission_case/unpaid-internships-are-discriminatory-and-should-be-ended-0, accessed 22 July 2013.

ways of working within the labour market and state systems. The strength of current career norms, which attach higher social status to what might be termed "traditional" careers (often office-based, "white collar" roles), have meant that some Edgeryders feel compelled to conform. They have taken jobs that are neither fulfilling nor developmental, and that are sometimes detrimental to their well-being, simply because opting for the lesser trodden path is fraught with even greater risk and uncertainty.

A second form of marginalisation exists in which Edgeryders' actions within (fairly) mainstream physical or virtual spaces are deemed "inappropriate" to that space by intervening authorities. While on the one hand this relates closely to the appropriation of public spaces described above, it was equally applicable to virtual spaces on the Internet. In a mission report entitled "Write or die", for instance, Nirgal reports being asked to remove his writing from a website he had been posting on.[34] In these circumstances Edgeryders' actions are pushed into more marginal spaces, reducing the impact they are able to have. If Edgeryders' work is continually pushed to the margins, blocked, or described as "inappropriate" by institutions, will disenchantment set in such that the innovative ideas demonstrably possessed by this group are never developed or exposed? Such an eventuality would result in young talent being wasted and potential solutions to social challenges being overlooked. This is as true for issues of funding as it is for access to spaces in which to act. The topic is discussed in more detail later in the report.

The risk that emerged most commonly – if sometimes implicitly – throughout the platform was that of failing to make a successful transition to an independent adult life. For some Edgeryders a constant preoccupation was whether there would be opportunities for family life in their future – would they ever achieve sufficient security to allow this? In one sense this would seem to be a private concern, and, as such, one which does not immediately attract public attention. Yet personal and family relationships, in particular, are closely linked with many other spheres of life, especially those related to employment, since family support can be fundamental to fulfilling career aspirations or expectations.

Most commonly, Edgeryders were concerned about achieving a transition that allowed them to pursue meaningful work. However, if gaining stability and security remains a priority for young people, and if these are increasingly difficult to achieve through available forms of work, do Edgeryders face a lifetime of precariousness? If this is the case, there are significant implications for state institutions, which may find themselves

34. Nirgal, "Share your ryde: write or die", available at http://edgeryders.ppa.coe.int/share-your-ryde/mission_case/write-or-die, accessed 22 July 2013.

with greater welfare bills for those unable to secure permanent paid work – indeed, this is already happening in the UK. There are two key issues to note here.

The first concerns the notion that existing norms surrounding the pathways to achieving stability and security are increasingly defunct. One Edgeryder describes "the idealistic view of how university translates into professional status",[35] emphasising the extent to which current economic circumstances have put an end to the time when a university degree was a guarantee of a secure career. Much discussion on the platform crystallised around a strong sense that today's formal education systems fail to prepare young people for the challenges they face when embarking on their key life transitions in the current socio-economic climate.

Some Edgeryders clearly feel considerable social pressure to conform to existing norms around stable employment and the lifestyles associated with these forms of work, but at the same time there exists a growing realisation that even the most historically stable forms of employment – so-called "jobs for life" – may themselves be increasingly tainted by uncertainty. Edgeryders seem to acknowledge the trade-off between stability (which is anyway fading fast) and fulfilling and meaningful work, but an overriding concern is the need to make enough money to live. Certainly they do not want to depend on state provision and entrench the view that young people are a social problem or national burden. As another Edgeryder, Edwin, says: "I don't want money for its own sake, but I don't want to get kicked out of my apartment either so I'll need some."[36]

The second issue concerns the problem of wasted talent. Nirgal writes:

> There are also millions of wasted talents ... I could write an encyclopedia about all the talents wasted because they just can't find their place or because they are not used for something good.[37]

The kinds of risks outlined above constrain young people's attempts to make use of their talents. This could result in an unfulfilled and disillusioned generation, and inhibit the ability of society to address its own problems by drawing on the talents, entrepreneurialism and enthusiasm of its young.

---

35. Noemi Salantiu in a comment on Di Bere's mission report, "Share your ryde: 'crossroads' sounds so cliche", available at http://edgeryders.ppa.coe.int/share-your-ryde/mission_case/crossroads-sounds-so-cliche, accessed 22 July 2013.
36. Edwin, "The quest for paid work: mo money, mo problems", available at http://edgeryders.ppa.coe.int/quest-paid-work/mission_case/mo-money-mo-problems, accessed 22 July 2013.
37. Nirgal, "Share your ryde: write or die", available at http://edgeryders.ppa.coe.int/share-your-ryde/mission_case/write-or-die, accessed 22 July 2013.

The forces that drive the most profound risks to young people's transitions are often embedded in institutional rules and norms. It is unsurprising, therefore, that Edgeryders feel that a gulf exists between their aspirations and world views, and the ways their lives are perceived by those institutions (that is, often in problematic terms). While the two do not generally come into direct conflict, the lack of understanding that maintains the gulf should be a cause for concern. The risk for policy makers and government institutions in particular is that young people will increasingly turn to "anarchic" politics and simply step outside the system.

4. Resources

In a mission report uploaded after the Living on the Edge conference, Charanya Chidambaram declares: "I am my own resource."[38] This comment underlines the extent to which Edgeryders not only recognise and value their skills, creativity and competences, as well as the autonomy these provide, but also realise that being one's own resource is fundamental to making the transition to an independent life today. However, while Edgeryders are clearly adept at acknowledging and making use of their own competences, they equally realise that, in order to move forward and have the results they desire, external resources are also needed. These resources take several different forms but the key connector linking them is people – people as allies and people as networks.

Networks emerged as one of the most significant themes across the project – such that a formal network analysis of the *Edgeryders* community has formed a key part of project research.[39] Networks – both real and virtual – constitute a fundamental support structure offering inspiration, motivation, tips and guidance, mentoring, technical information and emotional support. They are also the conduits through which ideas and innovations are communicated and money (sometimes) is generated. As such, they are the lifeblood of an individual's desire to "craft" a particular future. Further, it was clear that at a time of great instability, when more people are working autonomously, it is unfeasible to rely on the stability of institutions. Instead, Edgeryders rely on the stability provided by social networks, especially families and peers. This was particularly visible in the Unconference following Living on the Edge, which swiftly generated a working list of ways in which the *Edgeryders* community could develop outside the remit of the project itself.[40]

38. Charanya Chidambaram, "Where Edgeryders dare: paid work – challenges & path forward", available at http://edgeryders.ppa.coe.int/where-edgeryders-dare/mission_case/paid-work-challenges-path-forward, accessed 22 July 2013.
39. See the report of G. Marcus and B. Vickers, 2012.
40. Thejaymo, "Help build the June conference!: Edgecamp in a box – Starting local Edgeryders community groups", available at http://edgeryders.ppa.coe.int/help-build-june-conference/mission_case/edgecamp-box-starting-local-edgeryders-community-groups, accessed 22 July 2013.

In large part the stability from which Edgeryders drew support in their interactions with various networks was generated through a pervasive understanding of reciprocity. In an age of social media, it has never been easier to build a community suited to one's own requirements. Maintaining these networks in ways that result in positive feedback from peers and create work opportunities requires a commitment to reciprocity, in the sense of contributing and delivering on one's commitments, as well as benefiting. But doing so offers manifold advantages. In particular, in an online environment character-ised by collaboration and mutuality, and where reputation is everything being a good peer requires giving as much as taking. Edgeryder Jorge Couchet sums this up in his mission report "A world of peers", when he writes: "I'm dreaming of a world where we are all peers."[41] – and indeed there is a strong sense across the project as a whole that learning, working and collaborating at peer level offers a more dynamic, responsive, as well as equitable and sustainable form of work.

While peer networks play an important role in driving forward Edgeryders' projects, families are commonly the key allies even before this stage is reached. A large propor-tion of participants have written warmly and appreciatively of the support provided by family members throughout their transitions. Emotional support is, of course, a key component of this, but it often extends to other essential resources including accom-modation, food and money. Mission reports posted as part of the Living Together campaign have suggested that, for some Edgeryders, peer networks are taking on characteristics associated with families, in terms of the emotional support and solidarity they provide, and this is perhaps a reflection not only of our networked society but also of the increasing mobility of global citizens within and beyond Europe.

Families, however, remain the cornerstone of many Edgeryders' activities because of the often unconditional support they are willing to provide. The issue of financial support is worthy of particular discussion. For some Edgeryders, financial support (or support in kind such as living with parents rent free) from family members has allowed them to pursue work that inspires them, often by setting up ventures of their own with family "seed" money. However, present-day economic challenges mean fewer young people have access to family-based financial support through periods of study or sporadic employment. These young people have to balance making enough money to live on in the present with pursuing the opportunities that will hopefully build them a longer-term future, often while saving money to fund those opportunities. But for another group of Edgeryders, access to resources – from family members or other sources – is still much more problematic. While the Internet goes some way to alleviating this sort

41. Jorge.couchet, "Bootcamp: a world of peers", available at http:// edgeryders.ppa.coe.int/bootcamp/ mission_case/world-peers, accessed 22 July 2013.

of inequality, it should be remembered that Internet/ICT access is still far from available to all young people.

A key question remains, therefore, regarding whose responsibility it is, or should be, to provide the resources – and thus a fundamental part of the support system – that young people need to successfully make the transition to an independent life. Edgeryders' stories make clear that it is still the oft-cited triad of family, friends and fools that takes the risks to back their activities. Edgeryder Andrea Paoletti notes in his mission report, "The serial exploring co-designer",[42] that applying for funding can be a full-time job, and it can take time to accumulate enough money to pay for even a part-time fundraiser. In essence, it takes money (or at least resources of various kinds) to make money. In this sense, differences in access to credit, rather than being an outcome, are exacerbating existing social differences associated with unequal access. In light of the multiple benefits that Edgeryders' actions are already according to numerous individuals and communities, perhaps the fundamental question is: who else should be bearing the risks – and enjoying the rewards – of Edgeryders' initiatives?

Since this is a policy-funded and policy-focused project this question may be taken as rhetorical, yet the scant institutional support for youth initiatives makes it worth emphasising. There is a clear need for those in need of money and those with the money to communicate more effectively such that a more productive and efficient (maybe even collaborative) working relationship can be forged. Edgeryders and external funders must better understand one another's needs, abilities and limitations in order to allow both to do their jobs. During the Unconference that followed Living on the Edge, several Edgeryders collaborated on an open letter to funders which is as much a call to find new, more productive ways to work together as actually identifying and accessing funding.[43] Yet while actions such as this letter demonstrate commitment from participants to do their bit towards a more collaborative working relationship with institutions, a deeply entrenched institutional culture remains in place, and it frames conceptualisations of trust, risk, profit (or other social rewards) and reputation in terms that fail to accommodate Edgeryders' ways of conducting equally if not more legitimate business.

It should be acknowledged that Edgeryders possess very sophisticated knowledge of many institutional systems – business, government and civil society – but recurring

---

42. Andrea Paoletti, "Share Your Ryde: The serial exploring co-designer", available at http://edgeryders.wikispiral.org/share-your-ryde/mission_case/serial-exploring-co-designer, accessed 22 July 2013.
43. demsoc, "Help build the June conference!: Funding 2.0 Edgecamp session: 'Dear Funders' letter", available at http://edgeryders.wikispiral.org/help-build-june-conference/mission_case/funding-20-edgecamp-session-dear-funders-letter, accessed 22 July 2013.

comments across several campaigns concerned the extent to which this knowledge was self-sought and self-taught through experience. Particularly within the "Making a Living" and "Learning" campaigns, Edgeryders voiced concern about the inability of formal education systems to provide them with a grounded knowledge of how the "real world" works. While many expressed appreciation of their experiences of higher education, acknowledging its positive impact on the navigation of their transitions, there was considerable frustration that they were entering a labour market highly qualified yet unable to respond to the challenges posed by the current crisis. In her mission report, "There's gonna be some changes made", Adria Florea[44] argues that making use of resources, networks and allies is far easier for those who possess an understanding of how they fit into the bigger system, and she notes a major opportunity for innovation in this space. Some Edgeryders are already active here – higiacomo,[45] Ben Vickers[46] and andrealatino[47] have all developed services to support young people's post-education transitions. Nevertheless, there remains considerable scope for educational institutions to be creative about the support they provide to students.

5. Responses

Edgeryders' responses to their frustrations with society are characterised by the sort of innovative thinking that permeates many of the experiences shared in the course of this project. As one participant commented on a mission report in the Caring for Commons campaign: "Young people are supposed to be a problem category, but they actually display more initiative than the people who are supposed to help them!"[48]

Edgeryders naturally seek to implement their values in their own field of interest: Andrea Paoletti, for instance, a designer from the north of Italy who specialises in planning

44. Adria Florea, "First lessons in work: there's gonna be some changes made", available at http://edgeryders.ppa.coe.int/first-lessons-work/mission_case/theres-gonna-be-some-changes-made, accessed 22 July 2013.
45. Higiacomo, "The quest for paid work: passion->volunteer->job->... passion again?" available at http:// edgeryders.ppa.coe.int/quest-paid-work/mission_case/passion-volunteer-job-passion-again, accessed 22 July 2013.
46. Ben Vickers, "Spotlight social innovation: professional reality development", available at http://edgeryders.ppa.coe.int/spotlight-social-innovation/mission_case/professional-reality-development, accessed 22 July 2013.
47. Andrealatino, "Share your ryde: 'what we have done for others and the world remains, and is immortal'", available at http://edgeryders.ppa.coe.int/share-your-ryde/mission_case/what-we-have-done-others-and-world-remains-and-immortal, accessed 22 July 2013.
48. Alberto Cottica commenting on FelixWaterhouse's mission report, "We, the sharers: the housing estate – nexus of commons", available at http://edgeryders.ppa.coe.int/we-sharers/mission_case/housing-estate-nexus-commons#comment-1660, accessed 22 July 2013.

co-working space, has located the centre of his work activity in the deep south of Italy – a counterintuitive decision given the severe economic disadvantages faced by this area – and aims to encourage social innovation there. At one of the plenary sessions at the Living on the Edge conference, James, an artist and activist who runs a free, open digital lab which repurposes trash technology for the community, declared "paying is so last century", a statement that clearly resonated with many in the community, who re-tweeted it several times throughout the conference session. These examples are indicative of Edgeryders' commitment to realising their own projects, leaving behind traditional patterns of entrepreneurship and creating pathways which challenge established employment and money-making norms.

More generally, however, the focus is often on forward and collaborative thinking. LucasG writes:

> Thinking about next year, I think I need to look at the hard realities and start some kind of **dialogue** as to what to do next – where and how will be my questions … I guess I'll have to have conversations, join people who are already doing things, see why those who might are not doing things, and really find some leverage.[49]

Specifically, in practical terms Edgeryders seek to contribute to improving their lives, and those of their peers, by deploying their skills and resources in those contexts where they believe they can have meaningful impact. Here it should be noted that, in relation to previous generations, the lives of contemporary youth are often viewed as being characterised by the so-called individualisation thesis (Beck 1992; Giddens 1991), which postulates that each individual is in charge of his/her own destiny in a context in which no preconceived paths are given. A necessary tool with which to respond to this state of uncertainty is reflexivity, and, as the responses on the platform demonstrate, Edgeryders are adept at self-reflection: even when everything is running smoothly, Edgeryders question why and how,[50] as in Hexayurt's "The subtle art of precarity":

> Some parts of my experience are very individual – my life path is deeply unconventional and likely unique. Other areas are very typical – unable to manage both my personal cause and acquisition of the trappings of adulthood like a mortgage and a car, never mind the fruits of adulthood like children. I exist as a perpetual boy, my possessions not all that different from what I owned in my 20s, even as I approach the last weeks of my 30s.[51]

---

49. LucasG, "Share your ryde: my ride with local food", available at http://edgeryders.ppa.coe.int/share-your-ryde/mission_case/my-ride-local-food, accessed 22 July 2013.
50. As in Paola Lucciola's "Share your ryde: it's a problem of personal choices or of a lost generation?", available at http://edgeryders.ppa.coe.int/share-your-ryde/mission_case/its-problem-personal-choices-or-lost-generation, accessed 22 July 2013.
51. Hexayurt, "Share your ryde: the subtle art of precarity", available at http://edgeryders.wikispiral.org/share-your-ryde/mission_case/subtle-art-precarity, accessed 22 July 2013.

Or as in K's mission report "Prototyping environments and finding good peers":[52]

> Education has its dangers:
>
> – Get stuck in a subject bubble: when only your fellow researchers can understand what you're talking about. When studying is exciting there is a risk to become biased and to start collective polarisation amongst your fellow colleagues/classmates.
>
> The trick which works for me: to mingle as much as I can with those who study subjects different from mine and work in a different field. If I'm losing the ability to explain to them what I'm studying and why it is exciting, it is a stuck-in-a-bubble alert.

However, whilst Edgeryders are living the individualisation thesis, they are also subverting it through their desire for connectivity, community, collaboration and communication, and in this respect their response creates a noteworthy challenge to extant dominant theorisations of young lives.

It is also important to acknowledge that not only are Edgeryders' actions concerned with addressing socio-cultural needs in terms of everyday human welfare, they also consider the scope for economic gains to be made in circumstances where opening up access to knowledge, data and politics may act as an enabler of innovation and enterprise. Indeed, it should be emphasised that Edgeryders are not just desirous of taking action to form the sort of future they want: their action goes beyond activism and campaigning to actually providing the services they feel are needed but missing. They are actively setting out how they believe things should be done rather than following existing channels which merely communicate dissatisfaction. This reflects a sea change in terms of civic disgruntlement, one in which Edgeryders are increasingly able to appropriate commons and networks to provide for themselves and others, and do this by working around the state (since state institutions are often the source of the problem).

In the realm of political participation, for instance, there seems to be a general agreement that existing methods of participation in local and national politics could be improved with limited effort, if only institutions were more attentive to the emergent needs of citizens, particularly regarding means of communication and engagement. Edgeryders describe the limited success achieved in their attempts to contact politicians. There is clearly, therefore, significant difficulty in making one's voice heard through traditional politics. Certainly Edgeryders believe that state powers are not on their side – and that they continue to be viewed as a problem rather than part of the solution. This

---

52. K, "Reality check: prototyping environments and finding good peers", available at http://edgeryders. ppa.coe.int/reality-check/mission_case/prototyping-environments-and-finding-good-peers, accessed 22 July 2013.

can be directly inferred from the evidence that so many of them position their beliefs and actions in direct opposition to those of their home states. The "We, the People" campaign contains many mission reports which articulate these frustrations, including hexayurt's provocative post, "Is democracy broken?"[53]

6. Scale

If we want to change something we have to start from our own environment even if the challenge is very hard to achieve.

(Irene Fazio, "From local to global, and back!")

One of the most striking facets of the project as a whole has been the way in which Edgeryders' actions have mediated between local and global concerns. As such, the scale(s) on which they act constitute an important analytical focus. Edgeryders are demonstrably keen to act on a variety of scales – local, regional, national and international – and in both physical and virtual spaces. What is important to note, however, is that even those focusing their energy on local projects are generally doing so in response to global issues. A key question that emerged in the early analysis of this project concerned how these multi-scalar interactions knitted together (Marcus and Vickers 2012). Viewing the project in its later stages, a clear pattern could be perceived.

When it comes to detailed information on specific projects, the focus in the mission reports of participants is most commonly on geographically local action or local challenges. In one respect this is likely to reflect the fact that limited personal resources make scaling up action or broadening its scope extremely difficult, if not impossible. It is also important to acknowledge that differing national political systems and sensitivities will influence the levels at which young people are able to act. What has proven significant is the concentration of activity at local levels even amongst those Edgeryders with the means to act at higher levels within their national political contexts. Edgeryders' actions revolve around initiatives that strengthen communities, helping them reengage and invest in the places they inhabit, leading to stronger forms of citizenship. Alessandra's mission report, in which she introduces the Italian language school for migrants she co-founded – LiberaLaParola – is a prime example.[54] LiberaLaParola unites

---

53. Hexayurt, "Reactivating democratic institutions: is democracy broken, or only mainstream political parties?", available at http://edgeryders.ppa.coe.int/reactivating-democratic-institutions/mission_case/democracy-broken-or-only-mainstream-political-part, accessed 22 July 2013.
54. Alessandra, "Protecting and enhancing commons: la lingua come un diritto da condividere: scuola di italiano libera e gratuita LiberaLaParola", available at http://edgeryders.ppa.coe.int/protecting-and-enhancing-commons/mission_case/la-lingua-come-un-diritto-da-condividere-scuola-di-ita, accessed 22 July 2013.

migrants and locals in a context focused on learning and sharing, and in doing so also helps deepen cultural understanding across the two groups.

Of particular interest was the fact that although Edgeryders are demonstrably very mobile and willing to relocate when necessary, there was a form of place embeddedness that kept their focus on acting locally and engaging people in the immediate community, whether or not it was that individual's home community. Talking about his work with the community of a large, urban housing estate in London, Felix Waterhouse said:

> The best way to change an area is to allow the people living and working there to come together and affect change themselves.[55]

Focusing efforts on this scale allows Edgeryders to contribute directly to change in their communities and observe the positive changes as they emerge. Alberto Cottica summarised the benefits of concentrating action on a small or local scale:

> Now I only commit to arenas where I can see my personal contribution making a change, even small. I will not be a number anymore. Not because I dislike it (I had great fun) but because it. Does. Not. Work.[56]

A key driver of Edgeryders' actions is thus the efficacy they achieve through their contributions – both for themselves in terms of personal competence and, perhaps more importantly, for the communities within which they aim to effect change. Nowhere is this more vividly represented than in a series of conversations on the platform around the (un)Monastery[57] – a proposal for several Edgeryders to live and work together for a year in a small community with the aim of supporting local citizens in addressing serious socio-economic problems, from youth unemployment to homelessness and computer (il)literacy.

Within Edgeryders' commitment to acting locally in response to larger-scale issues, a desire to protect or enhance commons was a conspicuous connecting theme. Often this was explicitly place-based and there are several mission reports which present participants' efforts to enhance common spaces, including: Aubrey and Ginevra's "Wiki

---

55. Felix Waterhouse, "We, the sharers: the housing estate – The nexus of commons", available at http://edgeryders.ppa.coe.int/we-sharers/mission_case/housing-estate-nexus-commons, accessed 22 July 2013.
56. Alberto Cottica in a comment on a mission report by T_indignadx, "Share your ryde: how do we overcome the fear towards change? Call it magic!", available at http://edgeryders.ppa.coe.int/share-your-ryde/mission_case/how-do-we-overcome-fear-towards-change-call-it-magic, accessed 22 July 2013.
57. Edwin, "Mine becomes ours: a few of us, living together (somewhere) and changing things? the (un)Monastery", available at http://edgeryders.ppa.coe.int/mine-becomes-ours/mission_case/few-us-living-together-somewhere-and-changing-things-unmonastery, accessed 22 July 2013.

Loves Monuments"[58] project to reconnect communities with their local cultural heritage; Alessia Zabatino's two reports on the occupation of a historical Italian building by creative knowledge workers;[59] Augusto Pirovano and friends' "CriticalCity Upload", a "game of urban transformation" in Milan;[60] and SARCHA's "Athens Travelers", where young people provide tourists with an experience of the city "from within".[61] These examples testify to Edgeryders' efforts to promote cultural diversity and expression, as well as tolerance and understanding, across different groups of town or city inhabitants. There is a strong sense of local pride underpinning these actions which reflects the integrity that, as we discuss above, is a key driver for Edgeryders' projects.

While the initiatives Edgeryders have presented on the platform have tended to be firmly place based (even those primarily located in the virtual space of the Internet are usually tied to at least one physical location – a particular city, for instance), mobility has formed an essential component of the stories participants have told. Sometimes these stories have involved personal travel – moving between countries while growing up, or travelling independently to experience the world and embrace its diversity as a young adult. Edgeryders credit the opportunities presented by the mobility most Europeans are fortunate to possess with fuelling their enthusiasm for new discoveries, their creative thinking and problem-solving dispositions – it has opened their eyes to the cultural diversity of Europe and the wider world, and this seems to invigorate them to direct their efforts towards the community with which they feel strong affinities. However, their travels also serve to emphasise the difficulties faced by some young Europeans for whom movement across European borders is still problematic.

58. Aubrey, "Spotlight: the Internet as a common resource: Wiki Loves Monuments: cultural heritage upgraded", available at http://edgeryders.ppa.coe.int/spotlight-internet-common-resource/mission_case/wiki-loves-monuments-cultural-heritage-upgraded, accessed 22 July 2013; Ginevra, "Spotlight: the Internet as a common resource: Wiki Loves Monuments in a nutshell", available at http://edgeryders.ppa.coe.int/spotlight-internet-common-resource/mission_case/wiki-loves-monuments-nutshell, accessed 22 July 2013.
59. Alessia Zabatino, "The acknowledgement of social value: the legitimate illegality. Culture as commons; a journey through the Italian spaces occupied by knowledge workers" #1 and #2, available at http://edgeryders.ppa.coe.int/protecting-and-enhancing-commons/mission_case/legitimate-illegality-culture-commons-journey-through-0 and http://edgeryders.ppa.coe.int/protecting-and-enhancing-commons/mission_case/legitimate-illegality-culture-commons-journey-through-, accessed 22 July 2013.
60. Augusto Pirovano, "Protecting and enhancing commons: we create games for urban public spaces", available at http://edgeryders.ppa.coe.int/protecting-and-enhancing-commons/mission_case/we-create-games-urban-public-spaces, accessed 22 July 2013.
61. SARCHA, "We, the sharers: Athens Travelers: Athens as introduced by its youth. Individual trajectories are turned into 'in common' city explorations", available at http://edgeryders.ppa.coe.int/we-sharers/mission_case/athens-travelers-athens-introduced-its-youth-individual-trajectories-are-tur, accessed 22 July 2013.

The benefits of travel and international mobility expressed by so many of the participants constitute an urgent call to promote mobility for all young people within Europe. This is particularly important in light of the education and employment benefits offered by schemes such as Erasmus, which was in particular discussed in extremely positive terms on the platform. This is a great opportunity for policy makers to conduct their own analysis into the nature of Erasmus' success and how it might be developed to offer more support and new initiatives at a time when such structures are increasingly needed – both by young people and potential employers in need of appropriately skilled staff. In this respect, the Erasmus for Young Entrepreneurs programme (discussed by Madalinab90[62] and Daniela Cantir[63]), which offers mentorship through work experience with established entrepreneurs, would appear to be especially pertinent.

Finally, it is important to consider how Edgeryders connect their local actions with the global issues that inspire them. In one sense this is about making use of the networks of resources and collaborators that allow their projects to happen (discussed in detail above). The Internet and other digital technologies are, undoubtedly, the key connectors here. Furthermore, it is in the realm of online collaboration and digital participation that Edgeryders' actions are holding up a mirror to the government institutions they are working around – because it is usually a case of working around them, rather than working with or alongside them. While Edgeryders are demonstrably highly competent – and innovative – in their use of virtual spaces and digital tools to seek collaborators, find audiences, and so on, often their frustration with government and other formal institutions stems from the fact that institutional engagement via these tools lags far behind. Emiliano Pirovano articulates this eloquently when he says that government institutions in particular do not know "Policy 2.0".[64] "Policy 2.0" requires the bridging of local, regional, national and international scale issues through the digital tools Edgeryders are already adept at employing. Perhaps, therefore, there is something institutions could learn from Edgeryders' use of these resources in order to offer better support for young people's transitions, particularly when it comes to transparency and accountability.

Alongside this, it bears emphasising that Edgeryders' projects were consistently more durable in the context of community than political projects. It seems that Edgeryders see their efforts as having a greater impact and more enduring legacy if they bypass official

62. Madalinab90, "Share your ryde: creativity and a smile can change the world", available at http://edgeryders.ppa.coe.int/share-your-ryde/mission_case/creativity-and-smile-can-change-world, accessed 22 July 2013.
63. Daniela Cantir, "Share your ryde: studying in Brussels", available at http://edgeryders.ppa.coe.int/share-your-ryde/mission_case/studying-brussels, accessed 22 July 2013.
64. Emiliano Fatello, "Bootcamp: live not survive", available at http://edgeryders.ppa.coe.int/bootcamp/mission_case/live-not-survive, accessed 22 July 2013.

figures and get on with driving the change themselves. But policy makers should consider just how much more Edgeryders' social enterprises, businesses and community initiatives could do to address contemporary socio-economic challenges if they were boosted by institutional support, particularly (although by no means exclusively) funding.

Conclusions

Our aim has been to emphasise some of the commonalities and shared experiences within the *Edgeryders* community. On the one hand, this could be seen as too ambitious a task given the breadth of experience and diverse backgrounds of the participants. On the other, there are some common traits that bind this community together surprisingly well. The first of these is the desire of Edgeryders to shape the world through their own positive contributions, and to do this in collaboration with peers with whom they share goals, experiences and values. Further, despite the persistence of social and cultural differences, Edgeryders share perhaps the most significant common background, that of the Internet. This was most clearly illustrated at the end of the *Edgeryders* mini-conference in March 2012 in Strasbourg, when a small group of Edgeryders were invited to introduce themselves. One responded by saying that he "comes from the Internet", followed by another participant's declaration that she "come[s] from the Internet too". This shared location in the virtual sphere, which transcends geographical boundaries, contributes to a convergence of both aspirations and expectations. It sets the stage for how Edgeryders perceive their roles in society – and, importantly, it defines the terms in which they want to interact with institutions.

What is most strikingly evident from Edgeryders' accounts is their commitment to progress – both in terms of their personal life projects and within their societies. Sometimes compromise may be required, but, as several Edgeryders stress, every compromise has the potential to offer experiences that pay dividends in the future. Certainly, as part of the rhetoric of the individualised society, few expectations exist around the notion of obtaining a stable pathway:

> Try and fail is the only possibility we have to find our path. It is normal and it is absolutely right to fail. It is our society that is telling us that failing is for losers, but in fact it is just the way it has to be. Failing without changing, that is for losers![65]

> We need to create a much larger framework, and then systematically, and in our own idiosyncratic ways, design and build new ways within it.[66]

---

65. Comment by Andrea Guida on Di Bere's mission report, "Share your ryde: 'crossroads' sounds so cliché", available at http://edgeryders.ppa.coe.int/share-your-ryde/mission_case/crossroads-sounds-so-cliché, accessed 22 July 2013.
66. Comment by Markroest on Paola Lucciola's mission report "Share your ryde: it's a problem of ersonal choices or of a lost generation?", available at http://edgeryders.ppa.coe.int/share-your-ryde/mission_case/its-problem-personal-choices-or-lost-generation, accessed 22 July 2013.

The picture drawn by the participants is that of a far more complex transition to a full independent life than traditionally conceived by policy makers and institutions alike, and this mirrors recent theorisations by youth researchers (Miles 2000). The rhetoric surrounding individualised trajectories may, in fact, jeopardise the efforts of young people by masking the limitations and barriers that Edgeryders have articulated and diverting attention from the support they need. The reality is that Europe's young people do need institutional support (of various sorts) to realise their plans, and the competence and commitment they already display in the projects described through the platform confirm that they are worthy recipients.

We feel that it is important to reiterate that Edgeryders' projects are invariably characterised by two aims – both of which should be of keen interest to policy makers in the context of the current socio-economic turbulence. The first of these is about securing their own futures – successfully making the transition to an independent life that allows them to provide for themselves and their families through work that accords with their values of integrity, passion and autonomy. In light of current unemployment rates such innovativeness deserves to be rewarded with institutional support to expand successful projects and promote entrepreneurialism amongst the young. The wider social benefits in terms of increasing employment opportunities in local areas are clear. And this leads to the second aim of Edgeryders' projects – to make a positive difference to society in the course of securing their own transitions. It is interesting to note that the final campaign to be launched during the *Edgeryders* project was called "Resilience". Reflecting on the project (at least in its present phase), resilience seems the most appropriate term to encapsulate what the project findings reveal about the priorities of European youth.

Although participants in this project have represented a diverse set of backgrounds and experiences, they have also been a self-selecting group of privileged actors, which means that inevitably some voices are missing. Furthermore, the mission reports have been shaped by the questions posed within the campaigns and, as a result, Edgeryders' stories have usually been framed around the positive actions they are taking as they navigate their transitions. In short, it must be acknowledged that there is a risk of reading these stories in too positive a light. This is not to say that Edgeryders' actions are not important and valuable – certainly they are – but simply that in focusing on the "good news" stories, attention may be shifted too far from areas where institutions retain significant responsibility and need to be held to account. It should also not be forgotten that, whilst the game element of the project might galvanise forms of communication which foster creativity and smooth relations between individuals and institutions, the corollary of this is the potential for playfulness to inadvertently overshadow the seriousness of some debates. There are few direct complaints on the platform about key issues being mishandled; instead Edgeryders concern themselves with how they can contribute to addressing the problems.

In sum, this project has been successful in demonstrating the energies, ideas and commitment to contributing to social life shared by European youth; presenting bottom-up recommendations on youth policies by shedding light on existing successful projects; facilitating networking; and giving a sense of satisfaction and fulfilment to participants before and after the community conference in June 2012. However, having one eye on the main goal of the Council of Europe – social inclusion – one must recognise the risk involved in considering the material on the *Edgeryders* platform as representative of youth in Europe. This kind of passionate participation is far from being a widespread phenomenon and institutions such as the Council of Europe should take this on board and be alert to the risk that many European youth may simply step outside the system. Institutions should, therefore, use all means available (particularly through the Internet) to speak the same language as Edgeryders, as digital natives – many young people, after all, now "come from the Internet" – in order to keep the channels of communication open. *Edgeryders* as a project has shown that such communication is not only possible, but also immensely fruitful.

References

Arnett, J. (2007), "Suffering, selfish, slackers? Myths and reality about emerging adults", *Journal of Youth and Adolescence* 36(1), pp. 23-29.

Beck, U. (1992), *Risk Society. Towards a New Modernity*, Sage, London.

Beneito-Montagut, R. (2011), "Ethnography goes online: towards a user-centred methodology to research interpersonal communication on the internet", *Qualitative Research* 11(6), pp. 716-35.

Borg, M. et al. (2012), "Opening up for many voices in knowledge construction", FQS 13(1).

Bynner, J. and Parsons, S. (2002), "Social Exclusion and the Transition from School to Work: The Case of Young People Not in Education, Employment, or Training (NEET)", *Journal of Vocational Behaviour* 60(2), pp. 289-309.

Cavalli, A. and Galland, O. (1996), *Senza fretta di crescere. L'ingresso difficile nella vita adulta, Liguori, Napoli.*

Charmaz, K. (2006), *Constructing Grounded Theory: A Practical Guide Through Qualitative Analysis*, Sage, London.

Côté, J.E. (2009), "Youth identity studies: history, controversies, and future directions?", Furlong, A. (ed.), *International handbook of youth and young adulthood*, Routledge, London.

Dentith, A.M., Measor, L. and O'Malley, M.P. (2012), "The Research Imagination Amid Dilemmas of Engaging Young People in Critical Participatory Work", Forum Qualitative Social Research 13(1), pp. 1-17.

Esping-Andersen, G. (1999), *Social foundation of post-industrial economies*, Oxford University Press, Oxford.

Esping-Andersen, G. (1990), *Three Worlds of Welfare Capitalism*, Princeton University Press, New Jersey.

Giddens, A. (1991), *Modernity and Self Identity. Self and Society in Late Modern Age*, Stanford University Press, Palo Alto.

Glaser, A. and Strauss, B. (1967), *The Discovery of Grounded Theory: Strategies for Qualitative Research*, Aldine Publishing Company, Chicago.

Heinz, W.R. (2002), "Transition. Discontinuities and the biographical shaping of early work careers", *Journal of Vocational Behaviour* 60(2), pp. 220-40.

Hookway, N. (2008), "'Entering the blogosphere': some strategies for using blogs in social research", *Qualitative Research* 8(91).

Jones, S. (ed.) (1999), *Doing Internet Research: Critical Issues and Methods for Examining the Net*, Sage Publications, London.

Kelan, E. (2009), *The Reflexive Generation: Young Professionals' Perspectives on Work, Career and Gender,* London Business School, London.

Leccardi, C. and Ruspini, E. (eds) (2006), *A New Youth? Young People, Generations and Family Life*, Ashgate, Aldershot.

Lehmann, W. (2004), "'For Some Reason, I Get a Little Scared': Structure, Agency, and Risk in School-Work Transitions", *Journal of Youth Studies*, Vol. 7, No. 4, pp. 379-396.

Marcus, G. and Vickers, B. (2012), "Edgeryders: a network analysis", report to the Council of Europe, published online.

Miles, S. (2000), *Youth Lifestyles in a Changing World*, Open University Press, Buckingham.

Pinquart, M., Juang L.P. and Silbereisena, R.K. (2003), "Self-efficacy and successful school-to-work transition: a longitudinal study", *Journal of Vocational Behaviour* 63(3), pp. 329-46.

Turkle, S. (1995), *Life on the Screen: Identity in the Age of the Internet*, Simon & Schuster, New York.

Walther, A. (2006), "Regimes of youth transitions. Choice, flexibility and security in young people's experiences across different European contexts", *Young* 14(2), pp. 119-39.

White, R. and Wyn, J. (2008), *Youth and Society: Exploring the Social Dynamics of Youth Experience*, Oxford University Press, Melbourne.

Worth, N. (2009), "Understanding youth transition as becoming: identity, time and futurity", *Geoforum* 40(6), pp. 1050-60.

Wyn, J. (2004), "Becoming adult in the 2000s: new transitions and new careers", *Family Matters* 68, pp. 6-12.

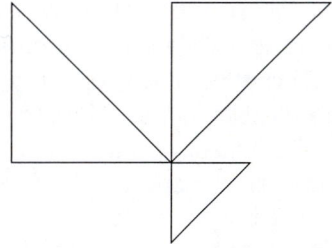

II. Transitioning into the future

Implications of what we learned from Edgeryders on policies and policy processes
Rebecca Collins

Introduction

There is widespread agreement that European youth are in a precarious position. Unemployment amongst under-25 year-olds is at its highest since the Organisation for Economic Co-operation and Development began keeping records, with rates in some countries (most notably Spain and Greece) exceeding 50%.[67] The pronounced split between northern and southern Europe, and western and eastern Europe in terms of youth unemployment rates (with the southern and eastern regions showing the highest numbers) illustrates how the consequences of the current global economic turbulence are hitting some groups particularly hard.

Economic challenges have precipitated a shift to increasingly uncertain working arrangements, and at the same time, there have never been more young people in search of a stable working life. With growing numbers of young people participating in tertiary (university) education, there has been inflation in formal educational qualifications (Gutiérrez-Esteban and Mikiewicz 2012) resulting in the perception that those with the means must remain in education for longer, accumulating more qualifications, in order to distinguish themselves within an ever-crowded job market. The result has been

---

67. www.oecd-ilibrary.org/employment/youth-unemployment-rate_20752342-table2, accessed 19 July 2013.

growing numbers of highly qualified young people chasing a series of short-term, poorly paid, low-skilled jobs. Accordingly, the term NEETs (Not in Education, Employment or Training) has been coined to describe those left on the very margins of society as a result of low social, cultural and/or economic capital. These young people are, perhaps more than any others, vulnerable to exclusion from social and political participation and denied opportunities for self-realisation (Bello 2012; Bynner and Parsons 2002).

To a large extent, the precariousness that currently characterises young people's lives is closely associated with these educational and employment challenges. However, they are by no means the only causes and consequences of this precariousness. Difficulties in accessing and affording housing is also a central feature, as are the effects of long-term insecurity on young people's personal relationships (especially with families, partners and children) and personal well-being (such as their ability to manage long-term stress). European youth are facing greater pressures and fewer opportunities at a time when there has also been growing political dissatisfaction. This has culminated in large-scale public demonstrations of frustration at governmental handling of a range of socio-economic challenges which have taken on international political significance. Yet there is also growing concern about the low numbers of youth participating in more traditional forms of politics, particularly party politics and direct involvement with civic institutions (Eriksson 2012). It would seem apparent, then, that contemporary youth feel very ambivalent about civic and political participation, and this could be read as either the result of, or their response to, the precariousness they face.

It is in this context that the *Edgeryders* project was devised as a means of deepening understanding of the specific challenges young Europeans feel they face in their attempts to successfully navigate the transition to an independent active life, as well as some of the innovative and creative ways they address them. *Edgeryders* is fundamentally premised on the construction of youth as part of the solution, rather than as an intrinsic social problem – a position that has, for some time now, been acknowledged as essential for the building of meaningful and effective youth-focused policies (Denstad 2009). As a project it has two closely related, interlinked aims:

—   to provide a space where young people from across Europe can share experiences of their transitions in ways that generate mutual support and understanding, and where solutions can be discussed and developed with like-minded peers;

—   to articulate where current policy is failing – either to understand the nature of young people's problems or to deliver appropriate solutions – and to offer their own ideas as to how institutions might be able to offer better focused and more effective support. In this respect *Edgeryders* aims to contribute directly to evidence-based policy making, which is widely promoted by European policy institutions but, as yet, remains infrequently implemented.

What is important to note is the interlinkage between these two aims. Much of the strength of *Edgeryders* as a project lies in its recognition of the power of collaboration and exchange. The conversations which constitute the project data have been spaces in which Edgeryders have, collaboratively, defined the nature of the challenges they face, frustrations they share and solutions they want to be part of.

There is an urgent need for social policy to take a progressive leap forward in order to proactively address the ways in which Europe's socio-economic problems are impacting on young people's lives. The young people who have become Edgeryders are demonstrably committed to engaging in action where they perceive social benefits and, as such, are ready to play their part. What they ask of institutions is to be given access to appropriate support mechanisms (discussed in "Call to action" part 4) in order to help them articulate the new social forms and cultural norms towards which society must collectively move.

The aim of this section is to present a range of Edgeryders' experiences as they have been expressed on the project platform[68] as a way of articulating the need for action in specific policy domains. The intention is to focus attention both on the most important policy themes (education, employment, access to commons, and so on) and on the ways in which policy is made and delivered in practice. In doing so, it is hoped that the points raised will inform the development of youth-focused policies which are not only well targeted and responsive to current challenges, but also characterised by methods of delivery in which citizens are actively involved rather than imposed upon.

Part one of this section introduces the *Edgeryders* community, describes who they are and why they and their experiences matter. This is followed by an overview of the youth policy landscape. This second part provides the context within which *Edgeryders* is situated and upon which it aims to have an impact. The third and main section of the report is entitled "Living on the Edge". Taking its name from the *Edgeryders* conference at which more than 120 Edgeryders gathered in June 2012, this chapter presents a range of project participants' own transition experiences as a means of illustrating some of the problems which characterise current youth-institution interactions. Part 4, "Call to action", constitutes a direct response to the issues raised at Living on the Edge. It sets out some of the ways in which institutional responses could simultaneously have a significant positive impact in smoothing Edgeryders' transitions and result in more effective policy outcomes generally. The conclusion reflects on what *Edgeryders*

---

68. http://edgeryders.wikispiral.org, accessed 19 July 2013.

as a project suggests about the future direction of youth policies, the extent to which the project has been successful as a citizen engagement mechanism, and how it has fulfilled aims beyond those directly concerned with informing future youth policies.

1. A European network of citizen experts

The lives of today's young people are characterised by a range of thorny socio-economic issues. These include: the emergence of new social structures as a result of changing work patterns; the growth of transnational mobility (often driven by the need to find work); the fragmentation of social groups as they have traditionally been defined; tokenistic efforts towards social inclusion for minority groups (see for example, Bello 2012); the enclosure of commons; and intergenerational inequality. As a result of these (and other) pressures, the widely acknowledged issue of precariousness now afflicts groups of young people who would not previously have been considered a cause for concern.

It is in this context that young people in Europe are experimenting with innovative solutions and thinking creatively about ways forward. What is important is that, by and large, they are taking this action peacefully and in ways that lead to the betterment not only of their own lives but of others of all ages, within and beyond their immediate communities. That they are able to achieve this in response to polarising large-scale political issues makes their actions worthy of respectful attention from those who would still see them as representing a problem to be solved.

Young people's responses to these politically pressing issues have tended to belie the social position they would be seen as inhabiting in "old" (arguably now redundant) social structures. In other words, class has less of a bearing on how young people are acting in the world; instead, values shared across class boundaries are the key determining factor. Participants in the *Edgeryders* project were, for instance, observed to engage in practices such as squatting (that is, occupying abandoned property) not out of financial need (the traditional driver, often experienced by the lowest class groups) but as a way of articulating the principles they want to live by: sharing, the right to a home, and revised concepts of property and value, to name but three. These principles are unequivocally based in the belief that outcomes bigger than fulfilling one's own present needs are at stake. Edgeryders' actions are, without doubt, based on common concerns and shared values, and are directed towards building a world that they want to be part of and contribute to.

Participation in *Edgeryders* has been wholly self-selecting. Edgeryders were not obliged to provide any personal information in order to participate and were free to remain fully anonymous, contributing to discussions under pseudonyms if they wished, although many contributed under their own names or otherwise identified themselves through information they shared in mission reports. The information Edgeryders shared about their age, education, careers, places of birth and residence, and so on was offered voluntarily in the course of their mission reports. Since the aim of the project was to cast the net wide as a means of eliciting the most diverse range of experiences possible, the participants are characterised by as many differences as similarities.

Few participants stated their exact age but a sense of each participant's stage in life tends to be evident from the experiences they share. The largest proportion of Edgeryders would seem to be those aged from their late teens to around 30. However, there have also been regular contributors in their 40s and 50s who have shared the same concerns as younger participants. Edgeryders are most commonly resident in the UK, Italy or France, but they come from 20 different countries and are extremely internationally mobile. There is huge variation in the nature of participants' careers or work experience depending on their age, countries inhabited, interests, education and skills. Indeed, some of the richest conversations on the platform addressed this topic.

On the whole, Edgeryders shared more similarities than differences. One of the most significant shared characteristics was education, or, perhaps more accurately, their attitudes towards learning. It is certainly not the case that all Edgeryders followed the same path and received comparable formal qualifications. However, there were two characteristics that Edgeryders seemed to share. First, the vast majority who mentioned their qualifications had attended university as undergraduates, with many having acquired, pursuing, or considering postgraduate study (Master's degrees or doctorates). Second, regardless of formal qualifications, there was a high intellectual standard displayed in the written content of the platform, which suggests a common level of intellectual capital gleaned from a range of both formal and informal educational sources.

In essence, although their educational paths are varied, Edgeryders are bright, articulate and skilled – in other words, they have high cultural capital. The fact that most speak at least two languages to a very high standard emphasises this.[69] A third key facet of this cultural capital is the ICT competence of Edgeryders. Since the gateway to participation in the project was a website, ICT competence (as well as access to the necessary technologies) was one of the few prerequisites for access. All Edgeryders were skilled in this regard, not only as demonstrated through their interactions on the platform but also through the resources, projects and initiatives that they discussed, and the networks they made use of. Indeed, often it was the latter that led them to the *Edgeryders* platform.

---

69. Although most mission reports were posted in English, there was no obligation to do so. Participants were invited to post in whichever language they felt most able to communicate their experiences.

As mentioned in the first section, the comments made by two participants at the *Edgeryders* mini-conference held in Strasbourg in March 2012 about belonging to the internet suggest that many Edgeryders consider the Internet the space in which they feel most able to act, connect and have impact. This shared location in the virtual sphere transcends geographical boundaries, facilitates mutual understanding and contributes to a convergence of both aspirations and expectations. It sets the stage for how Edgeryders perceive their roles in society – and, importantly, it defines the terms in which they want to interact with institutions. The location of *Edgeryders* in the virtual realm was what made research on this scale possible; the feasibility of doing so reflects the fact that, compared with the recent past, digital tools have made social and political participation much more accessible, particularly to the young.

While Edgeryders' geographical locations are relatively diverse, what they share is an ease with mobility – more Edgeryders stated they move between several European cities than stated they live in just one place. Furthermore, their mobility is not restricted to their physical location or movements; they are not only transnational in their mobility, but also trans-sectorial and trans-disciplinary (Potočnik 2012). This flexibility, combined with their apparently high cultural capital, means that Edgeryders could, in some respects, be described as a privileged group. However, in today's technology/media-mediated social context, the notion of "privilege" is itself in flux. A pressing task for social researchers (in both policy and academic domains) is a re-evaluation of what it means to be privileged in an age where growing numbers have Internet access but no job or economic security.[70]

Edgeryders has not explicitly aimed for representativeness in the sense of classic social research. The aim instead has been to be as inclusive as possible by making use of online tools to which growing numbers of young people, although admittedly not all, have access. This approach has offered the most time- and cost-effective means of reaching a large and disparate group in sufficient numbers to allow the project to draw robust conclusions.

The fact that some young people will inevitably have been excluded from the project because of the methodological choices made has not been overlooked; indeed, it is something the project team has remained acutely aware of. Since the scope of the first iteration of *Edgeryders* was unable to extend the research to engage these

---

70. A more detailed analysis of this topic is, regrettably, outside the remit of this report; however, see for example Jeffrey and McDowell (2004).

harder-to-reach groups,[71] one of the most important recommendations is the development of further work to fill this gap. This first version of *Edgeryders* could easily constitute a starting point, the findings of which could be tested with other groups.[72]

In summary, *Edgeryders* cast its net wide in order to engage a large and diverse group of young people who, more than any other characteristics that might link or divide them, are united by their shared experience of having to creatively navigate the transition to an independent active life in the most challenging socio-economic context in several decades. The group that emerged has produced a dynamic and illuminating space focused on the issues around which there is consensus that social and political change is most urgently needed.

2. Overview of the youth policy landscape

Reflecting the fact that socio-economic modernisation has taken different courses across Europe in recent decades, constructions of "youth" have also followed different paths and formed different patterns based on national mindsets and political discourses (Liebau and Chisholm 1993). As a result, cultural influences mean that, across Europe, there is no single definition of what "youth transition" means, what it involves, or how one goes about achieving transition successfully (McNeish and Loncle 2003; Walther et al. 2004; Walther 2006). European youth policy reflects this. Policies apply across national boundaries, having been formally agreed on and adopted by member states (Chisholm et al. 2011). They aim to formalise specific ambitions or agendas shared across Europe, while devolving responsibility for fulfilling these to individual nations. As such, national governments are tasked with devising initiatives which address the unique needs of their own young people, thus responding to Council of Europe guidance suggesting that: first, public policies should be anchored in the conditions and aspirations of the target group; second, these should align with the political objectives set by the respective public authorities; and third, policy responses should be differentiated in

---

71. That is, those who are low skilled and/or vocationally educated; those in rural areas with little access to civic institutions or consultative processes; those in eastern and southern Europe, of which there were few representatives in the platform (an exception being Romania, perhaps a reflection of the personal networks of the project team); citizens of non-EU member countries; and those who, for various reasons, are on the other side of the digital divide (Potočnik 2012). These groups also include those whose political activity is illegal or socially stigmatised, through for instance participation in riots and other forms of social unrest (Eriksson 2012). While not condoning these actions, it is no less important to understand the views and experiences of the young people who resort to these acts.

72. Members of the *Edgeryders* community are being invited to make use of the experiences they gained as part of this project by supporting other citizen groups to discuss and collaboratively build their own projects aimed at combating the kinds of precariousness specifically associated with exclusion.

response to the increasingly complex, unpredictable and vulnerable trajectories of contemporary youth (Siurala 2006).

It is clear that youth remain high on the agenda of both the European Union (EU) and the Council of Europe. Documents from the EU indicate as much:

- the White Paper, "A New Impetus for European Youth" (European Commission 2001), which aims to promote, in particular, active civic participation amongst youth;
- the European Youth Pact (Council of the European Union 2005), which re-emphasises the need to consult young people and their organisations on the implementation and follow-up of the pact at the national level;
- the recent *An EU Strategy for Youth – Investing and Empowering – A renewed open method of coordination to address youth challenges and opportunities* (Commission of the European Communities 2009); and
- the subsequent Resolution on a renewed framework for European co-operation in the youth field (2010-2018) (Council of the European Union 2009).

These communicate the EU vision for young people, which is based on two key aims: investing in youth, which means "putting in place greater resources to develop policy areas that affect young people in their daily life and improve their well-being" and empowering youth, which refers to "promoting the potential of young people for the renewal of society and to contribute to EU values and goals" (EUtrio.be 2011).

The Council of Europe has similarly made its commitment to youth clear in its report, "The future of the Council of Europe youth policy: Agenda 2020" (2008). This document outlines priority areas which include:

- promoting young people's active participation in democratic processes and every-day lives;
- empowering young people to promote cultural diversity and intercultural dialogue;
- ensuring young people's access to education, training and working life, particularly through the promotion and recognition of non-formal education/learning;
- supporting young people's transitions from education to the labour market;
- supporting young people's autonomy and well-being, as well as their access to decent living conditions.

While top-level aims and agendas are formulated at a transnational level, there is no universal approach to youth policy in Europe. The benefits of this flexibility in terms of allowing tailored responses to nationally specific needs are clear. However, it also carries with it a wide range of governance and delivery challenges, including management, monitoring, work force development and grant allocations. In order to ameliorate potential deficiencies in programmes and practice, an ongoing, open consultation process among policy makers, delivery agents and young people as constituents is essential as a means of ensuring resources are appropriately targeted. The whole process of youth policy creation, implementation, monitoring and evaluation, therefore, should be one of creative interaction among politicians and civil servants, professionals working in the sector (including youth researchers), and young people (not just youth NGOs). Best practice is only likely to emerge from a youth policy forged on the anvil of mutuality among these groups. In order to facilitate this, maintaining a strong network of key partners is essential (Siurala 2006), as is finding a common language through which to manage three-way co-operation (Williamson 2008).

It is clear, then, that within transnational European institutions there is top-level commitment to working together for common ends. Less obvious are the capacities of national governments to respond dynamically to national specificities. It has been noted by previous Council of Europe research (Williamson 2002) that all countries in Europe have a youth policy by intent, default or neglect, meaning that whatever a country may do or not do by way of its provisions for and practice with young people, its (in)actions inevitably have an effect on youth and their futures. The reality in Europe is that some countries do very little for young people (a policy of neglect), some may be reducing or diminishing their active focus on youth (a policy of default), while most of them frame policies purposefully on their behalf (a policy of intent). Furthermore, despite a shift in focus at the transnational level towards policies which encourage and promote young people's positive actions, some intentional policies remain preoccupied with the control and prevention of negative actions, such as behaviour deemed by institutions to be unacceptable, deviant or anti-social.

It has been suggested that five components are necessary for youth policies to move from political rhetoric and aspiration to impact and effectiveness:

1. Coverage – This refers to the geographical dimensions of social groups and policy issues. In spatial terms, how far does youth policy reach from the centre of administration? Do policy initiatives and measures actually reach all the young people at whom they are directed, especially when core objectives of particular policies are concerned with equalising opportunities or combating social exclusion? What is the "reach" of youth policy? Is it conceived within relatively narrow parameters, or does it embrace all those areas and aspects of policy that impinge on young people's lives?

2. Capacity – Do the structures exist to "make youth policy happen"? What are the relationships between central administrations and those at regional and local levels? Where does authority lie, and is it in the appropriate place for effective action? And what are the structural relationships between governmental processes and practices, non-governmental activity and youth organisations?

3. Competence – Do those in the youth policy field have the appropriate skills to deliver effective services? What is the relationship between professionals and "volunteers"? How do those working with and for young people build their knowledge, skills and attitudes – and keep them up to date?

4. Co-ordination/Co-operation/Communication – What is the nature of contact between different levels of administration and across different domains of youth policy?

5. Cost – The human and financial resources available for discharging the responsibilities of youth policy are essential for the generation of effective practice. A clear understanding of resource allocations and distribution, priority activities, and core and more discretionary budgets is necessary in order to permit the exploration of the four points above.

In light of the desire of policy makers to see young people become active citizens, the crucial question arises as to whether young people in transition have sufficient power and resources to accomplish all that is expected of them. Of paramount importance is the political championing of new agendas in response to the emergent needs of young people at this crucial stage. European research on change in young people's transitions from youth to adulthood in general, and from school to work in particular, largely agrees upon a diagnosis of ongoing de-standardisation, individualisation and fragmentation of transitions. This means that young people's biographical perspectives, their subjective appropriation of their own life courses, have to be taken seriously into consideration when formulating policy responses which will help rather than hinder their attempts to successfully navigate their transitions to independence. The diversification and uncertainty of biographical destinations related to the process of de-standardisation (magnified all the more in the present socio-economic context) tend to transgress the interpretative repertoire of national cultures and policy structures. This presents a further challenge to nation states as they attempt to legislate for transitions, especially in preventing and combating the risk of social exclusion.

Accordingly, understanding the complex, interlinked factors shaping the educational and labour market careers of young people in contemporary Europe, the unexpected ways that policy measures impact upon vulnerable youth and the difficulties of managing the interrelations and interdependencies among key youth policy areas (including education, employment and housing) should be a priority. At the same time, the growing and shifting impacts of globalisation, mobility, migration and democratic renewal (amongst other global social issues) emphasise the need to constantly review the aims, scope, nature and means of delivery of youth policies. Furthermore, and perhaps most crucially, youth policies must shift their energy from being reactive to proactive. If young people in Europe are genuinely seen as a resource for social renewal by policy makers, frameworks and support mechanisms which help them to live up to this role must be more readily forthcoming.

Edgeryders at the (cutting) edge of youth policy?

Denstad (2009) recommends that amongst other objectives, European youth policies should:

— involve young people both in the strategic formulation of youth policies and in eliciting their views about the operational effectiveness of policy implementation;

— establish systems for robust data collection, both to demonstrate the effectiveness of youth policies and reveal the extent to which "policy gaps"[73] exist in relation to effective service delivery to young people from certain social groups, in certain areas or in certain conditions; and to display a commitment to reducing such policy gaps where they demonstrably exist.

These are important points to note in light of the power of the Internet to aid participation and transparency. While policy makers have always, in some respects, been answerable to citizens through the governments they operate as part of (and for which citizens, to a greater or lesser extent, vote in elections), the Internet has expanded possibilities for unhappy citizens seeking to articulate their frustration, thus providing stakeholders in policy making with a more present voice. Not only can they watch more closely, they can comment (figuratively speaking) more loudly. Only a decade or two ago the journey of signals from the lived experience of policy back to the policy makers was slow and open to interference as a result of those signals being diluted by multiple intermediaries. Today, this feedback from citizens lands directly in the policy-making arena, with far fewer intermediaries (perhaps only a website). If institutional commitment to evidence-based policy making is genuine, young citizens will be watching to confirm or deny whether the evidence on which policy is based is true.

As a result of this greater visibility, it is easier to identify where there is wastage – in terms of money, effort and human potential. One of the biggest threats to the ability of Europe to thrive in coming decades is what is happening to its young people in the current economic turmoil. If it is true that the way in which youth is conceptualised

---

73. The overall assumption is that a youth policy will fulfil the needs of young people and that all young people will be fully equipped to meet the challenges of adulthood. This is a utopian assumption, and there will be weaknesses in any policy designed to meet those needs. It is shortfalls like these in the effectiveness of policies which are referred to as "policy gaps" (Williamson 2008).

in youth policy has shifted from youth as problem to youth as solution or resource, it is essential that these resources not be wasted or neglected or addressed with inappropriate policies. One of the primary aims of this report, and the *Edgeryders* project as a whole, is to provide the policy audience with insights which could help to reduce, and even eliminate, the wasted potential of young lives, as well as other forms of waste which result from the inefficient dissemination of institutional resources. The urgency of this is well expressed by one of the project participants, James:

> We realise now that the most valuable technology that is being discarded by our society is PEOPLE. We are seeing talented, skilled people unmobilised, and we think that this is a criminal waste. We also see deeply uninspiring, value-free jobs (like working in call centres) as the only structural answer put forward by mainstream business and industry, and we want people to work with us to develop more inspiring, creative, engaging, and socially valuable jobs as an alternative.[74]

The question emerges around which face a supra-national youth policy should have in order to formulate national youth policies which are acceptable for the governments of the (present and future) EU member states. It is important to note that at a European level youth issues enjoy perhaps a higher profile through the EU and the Council of Europe than they do in many national contexts. As such, it is essential that these and other transnational institutions remain drivers and supporters of well-researched, well-devised and well-targeted youth policies. More than this, however, it will be vital to go beyond commitments to structured dialogue between youth and institutions, as outlined in the European Commission White Paper on Youth[75] (and reiterated in the renewed framework) (Devlin 2010), to a system based on ongoing consultation, collaboration and involvement. Doing so will positively impact on institutional ability to devise youth policies that actually achieve the desired results. This is particularly important since one of the most significant challenges for policy makers is the fact that many areas outside of the traditional concerns of youth policy influence young people's attitudes towards the political sphere. This is well illustrated by Edgeryders' experiences, as revealed through their mission reports in the project platform. The following chapter, "Living on the edge", presents some of these experiences and highlights instances in which policy support was most crucially felt to be missing or misplaced.

---

74. James, "Spotlight: social innovation: access space, a new model for individual and community development", available at http://edgeryders.ppa.coe.int/spotlight-social-innovation/mission_case/access-space-new-model-individual-and-community-development, accessed 22 July 2013.

75. European Commission White Paper on Youth, "A New Impetus for European Youth" (2001); see also the Committee of Ministers Resolution (98) 6 on the youth policy of the Council of Europe and the Council of Europe Parliamentary Assembly Recommendation 1437 (2000) on non-formal education.

3. Living on the edge

In June 2012, over 120 Edgeryders from across Europe gathered at the Council of Europe in Strasbourg to engage with policy makers face to face. Taking its title from the name of this event, this chapter presents four areas in which Edgeryders' experiences can be a source of inspiration for with existing policy structures. It has been suggested that "[y]oung people are highly positive towards democracy, although they are often critical towards the way institutions work" (Titley 2008). Thus the challenge for youth policy is perhaps less about encouraging participation amongst youth (although for certain groups this may remain relevant) than about finding a way to align the work of institutions with the expectations and practices of today's young people in order to regain legitimacy amongst them. This chapter draws directly on Edgeryders' experiences in order to shed light on how and why a critical stance towards institutions has developed amongst European youth. The topics to be discussed here are the value of work , the elements that can make the difference, the mechanisms to establish trust and the need to develop new cultural norms.

3.1. Realising value in work, in education, in communities

It is clear from the nature of Edgeryders' precariousness that one of the fundamental points of friction with policy makers concerns what constitutes work of value. This extends far beyond young people's (precarious) place in the labour market to issues including: how different professional skills are valued, and by whom; the notions of value associated with different forms of education (or learning), and whether this value is perceived in personal (intellectual) or economic terms; and the extent to which unpaid work within communities should be valued monetarily.

Realising value in work

One of the most significant problems for Edgeryders is the fact that existing policies and labour market norms fail to value contributions to society (and thus, directly or indirectly, the economy) that do not conform to current definitions of "work". One contributor, Edwin, described the very different situations of two friends: one who is viewed positively by the government for being in work (despite the fact that the nature of that work may result in the need for government spending on foreign aid and mediation); the other who is threatened with withdrawal of his welfare payments if he does not give up his unpaid work running a community cinema to take up a menial job in retail.[76] Withdrawing financial support from those who work to improve social

---

76. Edwin, "Mo money, mo problems", available at http://edgeryders.ppa.coe.int/quest-paid-work/mission_case/mo-money-mo-problems, accessed 20 July 2013.

cohesion and well-being (work which is rarely acknowledged as valuable through the creation of paid roles) actively devalues efforts to improve communities and marks out these individuals as a problem to be solved rather than a welcome (relatively low- cost) solution. Edwin writes:

> We need to stop fetishising paid work, and value socially-minded productivity more. That means we need a new way to value a productive human hour – not just the current measure, which is the hourly wage.

He argues for the need for better support for "informal work" than the:

> current, informal one (which provides very little security), where young people must survive, sometimes for years, on grants or benefits whilst doing wonderful things for others. What about a low, guaranteed wage for full-time community workers, or something similar?

Having their work devalued by being told it is not the "right sort" of work is by no means the only problem Edgeryders face. The precariousness of young people is both taken advantage of and exacerbated by the recent growth in short-term, unpaid or low-paid internship or work experience placements. There are two main issues here. First, this fragmentation of the transition into work through the proliferation of short-term employment opportunities is flooding the labour market with a new form of "portfolio" worker whom, paradoxically, the market also seems unable to accommodate. Both public and private sector organisations are implicated as a result of current preferences for flexible contract working arrangements which keep the cost of employment down and mean staff numbers can be rapidly reduced at times of greatest economic difficulty. However, the transitory experience of work experienced by contract employees is causing major problems in a crowded labour market. One Edgeryder, Charanya Chidambaran, describes how short-term work opportunities have led to the emergence of young people who possess cross- or multi-disciplinary skill sets – what Charanya describes as "hybrids" and what other Edgeryders have discussed in terms of "portfolio" career workers.[77] While in one sense these might be viewed as offering an advantage in the current context, Charanya articulates the problem, also reported by several other Edgeryders, by noting that "society favours classical titles and hybrids fit none making it difficult for them to find a place in the traditional job market."

---

77. Charanya Chidambaran, "Where Edgeryders dare: paid work – challenges and path forward", available at http://edgeryders.ppa.coe.int/where-edgeryders-dare/mission_case/paid-work-challenges-path-forward, accessed 20 July 2013.

Anca Magyar's mission report revealed her first-hand experience of this frustration:[78]

> I have been told I have too much experience, I have been told I do not have any, I have been told I am too young or too old. I have been told I am way ahead of myself to be applying for a certain job, or not courageous enough to apply for another … I have been applying for jobs for 8 years in 3 countries and honestly I don't have a clue what recruiters want.

In essence, both public and private institutions are complicit in creating a new form of worker whom they then seem unable or unwilling to recruit.

The second circumstance in which young people's precariousness is being taken advantage of specifically pertains to the implications of unpaid and low-paid work experience in terms of social inequity. Edgeryder IdilM explains:

> I remember feeling absolutely scandalised and disgusted when the head of a UN organisation who had come to give a careers talk at our university early on in the year, when asked about the culture of unpaid internships in the organisation, replied in a blasé manner that "we expect your parents to pay" … This reeks of hypocrisy especially when the same organisation is claiming to fight poverty and social injustice across the world. So, whilst my colleagues were doing internships in Brussels and the Hague over the Easter break thanks to the bank of mum and dad, others like myself were denied these same opportunities by being inadvertently excluded through the unpaid internship schemes run by many governmental, intergovernmental and non-governmental organisations.[79]

In a labour market flooded with young people desperate to secure permanent work, there is no shortage of highly qualified candidates for institutions to choose from for their internship programmes. However, those most able to take up these opportunities for little or no pay are those whose (families') social and economic capital is able to support them. For those without these resources, these opportunities remain out of reach or are only available at high personal cost, necessitating either taking on debt or risking personal health and well-being by taking on paid work alongside the unpaid work.

Realising value in education

A similar problem exists when it comes to education – or what might be better described as pathways or spaces of learning. Much discussion within the "Making a Living" and "Learning" campaigns featured on the *Edgeryders* web platform concerned the extent to which current formal education systems prioritise forms of learning that fail to meet

---

78. Anca Magyar, "Surviving recruitment: advantage this disadvantages", available at http://edgeryders. ppa.coe.int/surviving-recruitment/mission_case/advantage-disadvatages, accessed 22 July 2013.
79. IdilM, "The quest for paid work: unpaid internships are discriminatory and should be ended", available at http://edgeryders.ppa.coe.int/quest-paid-work/mission_case/unpaid-internships-are-discriminatory-and-should-be-ended-0, accessed 22 July 2013.

the needs of today's young people. There was a widespread sense in particular that university had a role to play in preparing students for the "real world", including today's highly competitive labour market, yet the consensus was that this role was far from being fulfilled. Amalia Elena, for instance, writes:

> It's quite obvious that doing the basic mandatory studies isn't enough anymore. We live in a very competitive and dynamic world, which changes every day. For this reason, I firmly believe that we should do our best to acquire all necessary skills in this globalised world. But which are those skills? ... Who can help us acquiring those skills which we need so much? Well, up to a certain point, school of course. I mean, particularly those technical skills. But, school is not enough. It's not enough for technical skills and it's clearly not enough for Important Skills or for Soft Skills.[80]

Yet young Europeans feel compelled to stay within formal education systems, in part because of the resounding message from those systems and potential employers that formal education is a necessary requirement for the transition to an independent life, but also because at present there is simply no place for them in the labour market. At the same time, the old guarantee that formal qualifications constitute the passport to a successful and stable career is fast disappearing. The message currently being sent by the job market, where a large proportion of graduates are precariously employed in short-term, low-skilled jobs, is quite to the contrary.

Some Edgeryders felt at a loss to know how to acquire the skills they need to give themselves the greatest chance of achieving stability. Others had already begun to explore how to fill their knowledge gaps by taking innovative approaches to alternative forms of learning. Edgeryder Higiacomo was one of the most outspoken critics of current formal education systems:

> Twenty years at school didn't teach me how to: ... Face complex situations / setting the problem... Where and how I learnt it: The first work experience I had taught me there's no pre-defined solution for everything.[81]

Higiacomo's response was to develop an online repository for video courses to supplement the materials provided by his university, and since then he has devised an online career guidance service. Another Edgeryder, Ben, has developed a course module called "professional reality development" which provides an innovative space within formal

---

80. Amalia Elena, "Reality check: basic skills, V.I.S. & soft skills", available at http://edgeryders.ppa.coe.int/reality-check/mission_case/basic-skills-vis-soft-skills, accessed 22 July 2013.
81. Higiacomo, "Evaluation broke education", available at http://edgeryders.ppa.coe.int/reality-check/mission_case/evaluation-broke-education, accessed 22 July 2013.

education to discuss the transition to "real life" outside university.[82] There is evidently a growing need on the part of young people for support from institutions during this phase, and there is scope for universities to add value to the higher education experience by acknowledging and responding to this.

There may, however, be one further barrier to the expansion of these kinds of support mechanisms. The Edgeryders who are already active in plugging the learning gaps in higher education – such as Higiacomo and Ben – are making considerable use of peer learning, support and collaboration. The idea of sharing in formal education tends to be viewed with suspicion and is avoided because collaborative working makes it difficult to conduct formal assessments of individual performance, which current educational norms view as the best means of evaluation. Yet collaboration and idea sharing are increasingly a fundamental part of what drives innovation. Furthermore, learning is nowadays less about preparation for a specific career and more a means of ensuring personal flexibility and resilience in an increasingly uncertain world. There is, therefore, a growing need for formal education to value and actively nurture forms of learning – especially those rooted in collaboration – that are better able to prepare young people for the world they must inevitably navigate. In essence, sharing as a means of learning needs to be reframed as something to be encouraged rather than discouraged.

Realising value in communities

It should be understood that Edgeryders are not just concerned about how their own skills, competencies and contributions are valued. They are equally concerned with how the notion of value is attached (or not, as the case may be) to common resources – buildings, monuments, public spaces, nature and human potential. A particular preoccupation of some Edgeryders has been re-opening access to public buildings. Alessia Zabatino, for instance, provides detailed accounts of how theatres around Italy are being opened up for community use: for classes, workshops, talks and discussions, barter markets, childcare and entertainment.[83] The key point shared by Edgeryders working to re-open access to these common spaces is one of a double crisis of waste: first, the resource (whether a building, public square or rural green space) itself is being wasted

---

82. Ben, "Spotlight social innovation: professional reality development", available at http://edgeryders.ppa.coe.int/spotlight-social-innovation/mission_case/professional-reality-development, accessed 22 July 2013.
83. Alessia, "The acknowledgement of social value: the legitimate illegality culture as a commons. A journey through the Italian spaces occupied by knowledge workers" #1 and #2, available at http://edgeryders.ppa.coe.int/protecting-and-enhancing-commons/mission_case/legitimate-illegality-culture-commons-journey-through-0 and http://edgeryders.ppa.coe.int/protecting-and-enhancing-commons/mission_case/legitimate-illegality-culture-commons-journey-through-, accessed 22 July 2013.

through lack of use; second, human potential is being wasted as a direct result, since people are unable to access resources that they could otherwise bring into productive use, stimulating local economies and improving community well-being and cohesion. Commenting on a mission report by Jody on the million empty homes in the UK, Alberto Cottica writes: "It is hard, especially in a crisis-ridden country, to justify such a waste."[84]

While in some countries public administrations seem content to overlook the actions of groups that attempt to return commons to public use, in others Edgeryders risk criminalisation in response to their attempts to work for public benefit. It is clear that economic (property) value is being privileged over social value. What remains unacknowledged by regional administrations, it seems, is the amount of local benefit that arises from access to these spaces, without the need for direct input from those institutions themselves. Indeed, often it seems that work goes on when requests for support from public administrations are ignored.

In one sense, public administrations could be seen as inhibiting the potential for their cities to develop new modes of economic prosperity. This is something that Edgeryders are all too familiar with, as they too find their opportunities to develop their own economic prosperity constrained by current policies. In frustration at the apparent inability of governments to acknowledge the different forms of value created by community activities, Edgeryders are participating in several other informal economic systems which do acknowledge this work. Examples are barter currencies (local currencies which directly stimulate local economic exchange) and time banking (local currencies where the unit of exchange is one hour of work). Edgeryder Neodynos underlines the benefits of these systems beyond the acknowledgement of the labour they represent:

> They offer economic development options amidst all the current economic collapse and high unemployment, potentially also triggeri[n]g a revival of the formal economy.[85]

Means of stimulating the formal economy from a grassroots community level should be an important topic for reflection in policy circles, since economic concerns remain on top of their agenda.

---

84. Comment by Alberto Cottica on a mission report by Jody Boehnert, "Protecting and enhancing commons: 1,000,000 empty homes in the UK – authoritarian or co-operative housing?", available at http://edgeryders.ppa.coe.int/protecting-and-enhancing-commons/mission_case/1000000-empty-houses-uk-authoritarian-or-co-operative-, accessed 22 July 2013.
85. Neodynos, "Spotlight social innovation: alternative currencies to the rescue?", available at http://edgeryders.ppa.coe.int/spotlight-social-innovation/mission_case/alternative-currencies-rescue, accessed 22 July 2013.

How are Edgeryders realising value?

It is evident that there is considerable disparity between the perception of value within the current norms of the labour market, formal education, and local or regional government, and the ways in which Edgeryders want to contribute – and are contributing – to society. Edgeryders are creating and working within their own regimes of value – whether through innovating new ways of learning or meeting their material needs through bartering. They are drawing attention – peacefully but visibly – to where there is conspicuous waste in present systems by re-opening access to abandoned resources, and to instances in which policies are simply contradictory, such as the state encouraging community cohesion yet withdrawing support for those working towards these ends.

What is needed is a post-ideological institutional consensus on the definition(s) and meaning(s) of value, thus avoiding contradictions. Framing both economic and social value in more expansive and flexible terms would make a significant contribution to reducing the prevalence of waste in present systems. Doing so would not only make policy delivery mechanisms more efficient, but also accommodate the kinds of values and priorities – such as co-operation, community development, democratic participation and sustainability – on which Edgeryders are already basing their actions.

3.2. Making things happen

Edgeryders like to make things happen swiftly and efficiently. Sometimes this is through necessity; their precariousness requires quick action in order to ensure an income, a means of tapping into a new network, or simply somewhere to live. In other cases Edgeryders want to make things happen because of frustration that nobody else seems willing or able to; this can involve anything from bringing public buildings back into active use to providing career support services for students leaving university. Whatever the circumstances, Edgeryders want to act now and seek others in search of the same ends in order to realise their projects efficiently. The following sub-sections describe some of the ways in which Edgeryders are making things happen for the benefit of others, as well as themselves, with a discussion of the institutional barriers that inhibit their success.

Aggregating individuals

Most Edgeryders would contend that collectives of individuals can make things happen faster and more efficiently than bulky institutions – and several contributors offer evidence of this. Alberto Cottica, for instance, presented Spaghetti Open Data, a website which aggregates public data for public use.[86] While Spaghetti Open Data took around two months to build using wholly voluntary labour, it was over a year before the national government followed suit with its own open data portal.

Open source communities (Wikipedia being the best known example) offer prime evidence of the power of aggregated individual effort in instigating huge projects – and seeing them through to completion where a formal "end" point is intended – achieving more faster and on a larger scale than a single (large) organisation would be able to manage. That this is possible is thanks to the organisational and participatory powers of the Internet. Yet despite the fact that open source communities have been established as efficient mechanisms "making things happen" for a number of years,[87] and despite their demonstrable efficacy in achieving their stated objectives, funding for projects remains heavily weighted towards established institutions – described in conversations among Edgeryders as "those with a letterhead" – rather than newer, more innovative, and more dynamic organisational forms. In other words, there appears to be a deeply entrenched bias towards assumptions of institutional efficacy over individual (networked) efficacy.

The apparent lack of trust between these two organisational forms is severely inhibiting the ability of both to achieve their respective aims. Building this trust requires willingness to engage in a productive working relationship built on openness and collaboration. Edgeryders who are active in open source community ventures, as well as other forms of social innovation, need institutional support for non-institutionalised transnational collaborations. Mechanisms are required to help individuals, small groups and networks address large-scale problems, and funding streams which allocate funds to non-institutional bodies or projects should form a central part of these. Edgeryders are demonstrably keen to play their part in helping institutions understand their aims, ambitions and modes of operation, and this was best articulated in a letter to potential funders written by participants in EdgeCamp, a two-day event which followed the *Edgeryders* conference in June 2012.[88] The full text of the letter can be found in Appendix B.

---

86. Alberto Cottica, "Hacking for change: Spaghetti Open Data: a little thing that feels right", available at http://edgeryders.ppa.coe.int/hacking-change/mission_case/spaghetti-open-data-little-thing-feels-right, accessed 22 July 2013.

87. Neodynos suggests that open source communities have existed for as long as computer programming has existed, but notes that growing access to open source hosting and other tools in the last 10 to 12 years has had a significant impact on its proliferation (comment on Beckery's mission report "The history of open source communities", available at http://edgeryders.ppa.coe.int/making-sense-edgeryders-experiences-where-do-we-go-here/mission_case/history-open-source-communities, accessed 22 July 2013.

88. Demsoc, "Funding 2.0 Edgecamp session: 'Dear Funders' letter", available at http://edgeryders.ppa.coe.int/help-build-june-conference/mission_case/funding-20-edgecamp-session-dear-funders-letter, accessed 22 July 2013.

Openness, understanding, accountability

The difficulties Edgeryders report in accessing funding or other kinds of support suggest that there is some anxiety amongst institutions about the level of risk involved. These anxieties could be reduced through more open and collaborative conversations between those seeking support and those with support to offer, with the result that funders better understand what they are being asked to support and perhaps feel reassured by evidence of existing success. This kind of communication not only helps projects to progress more rapidly, the development of individual relationships along with greater transparency means all parties are more accountable, and are incentivised to perform in order to maintain reputations.

The need for greater openness is not confined to funding. There are other ways in which openness can have significant benefits, not only for Edgeryders' projects but also wider communities and their relationships with administrative institutions. Open data – where institutional data is made available for public consultation – is a key example which received considerable attention on the *Edgeryders* platform. Open data helps groups or individuals take action of their own accord, allowing citizens to engage directly with political institutions on issues that matter to them, rather than interacting sporadically with government representatives. Edgeryder Demsoc articulated the value of this to citizens in the context of an open data network mapping initiative called We Live Here:

> People don't think about "democracy", they think about needs. Although people felt that there were issues that they wanted to raise with the council and with public services, the civic activists we spoke to were largely uninterested in "democracy" conceptually. They were interested in getting solutions to community needs, and expressing community voices – goals that actually would need to be delivered by democracy.[89]

Not only do citizens have the right to follow the work of their local administrations in real time in order to hold them accountable, open data can equally be seen as a means of co-operation between government and citizens to create better services. The data may be used by small citizen initiatives in more agile ways than institutions. As Alberto Cottica suggests:

> With open data it seems quite clear that hacktivists and civil society organizations are just way better and faster than government agencies in performing some of the related operations ... You would think institutions might react badly, but so far they actually liked it a lot. I think what is happening is this: civil society is emerging as an ally of the innovators within the public sector. They can go to their bosses and say "look, these guys are

---

89. Demsoc, "Reactivating democratic institutions: networking the networks", available at http://edgeryders.ppa.coe.int/reactivating-democratic-institutions/mission_case/networking-networks, accessed 22 July 2013.

hell bent on this stuff. Either we move fast or they will move first and leave us looking like idiots. The good news is, we can ask them to help us, and they will! So we can appropriate some political benefit releasing data, and everybody wins."[90]

While there is much talk in both public and private sector circles about the balance to be struck between top-down and bottom-up approaches to engaging with the public, Edgeryders are employing approaches that are best described as "from-the-middle-and-out". One Edgeryder, Pedro, presented an initiative called Kyopol, a system which uses the Internet as a catalyst for civic engagement and citizen action:

> Kyopol promotes the development of "high quality" civic initiatives, by providing tools, methodologies and teaching resources that promote a participation which is transparent, informed, balanced, profound and documented ... Kyopol works, in short, as a decentralized and transparent "Facebook of civic engagement", which would be regularly used by citizens and institutions of all kinds, to inform (/inform themselves) about civic initiatives taking place in the places they care for, and deal with subjects that matter to them.[91]

These multiple ways of creating more openness between institutions and citizens both empower citizens to find and act on their own solutions to community needs, and offer a foundation on which institutions can build their own information-sharing initiatives. What is needed as far as Edgeryders are concerned is more active instigation of these activities and relationships by institutions, as well as more support for initiatives developed outside of institutional walls. One of the tools which might increase the willingness of institutions to invest funding in community-developed projects is the use of models, tried-and-tested scenarios or "prototypes".

Prototyping projects

Prototyping offers the creators of projects a means of testing the feasibility of their ideas, working out the capacity for those ideas to be scaled up, eliciting feedback, and gaining acknowledgement of success as their project grows and is developed in new locations. Often the projects Edgeryders have devised or are part of constitute a prototype – an initiative that they hope will grow in impact but which requires refinement, as well as more investment. Securing this investment is often the most difficult part. Yet some Edgeryders are involved in initiatives that prototype new forms of living and working

---

90. Alberto comments on his mission report, "Spaghetti Open Data: a little thing that feels right", available at http://edgeryders.ppa.coe.int/hacking-change/mission_case/spaghetti-open-data-little-thing-feels-right, accessed 20 July 2013.

91. Pedro, "Share your ryde: creation of Kyopol System (aka: 'Symbiotic City'): the Internet as a catalyst for civic engagement and citizens' activation – ckyosei.org", available at http://edgeryders.ppa.coe.int/share-your-ryde/mission_case/creation-kyopol-system-aka-symbiotic-city-internet-catalyst-civic-engag, accessed 22 July 2013.

and have been able to secure institutional support. The best known of these is the "Transition Towns" movement, which aims to support communities in increasing their resilience to economic and environmental shocks.[92] While Transition Towns are community initiated and led, they are often able to gain support from local municipalities. In part this seems to stem from their ability to take a holistic systems perspective of the interactions and exchanges in a town and recognise how all stakeholders have a part to play in the "transition".

The notion of a Transition Town was itself once a prototype (in Totnes, Devon, in the UK) and is now a successful and growing global movement. However, its innovative stance on what a community could be needed local institutional legitimacy and support in order to thrive. Innovation in all its forms requires a similar approach – one where ideas are given space to flourish organically, rather than prescribed in ways which extinguish creativity. It is also important to acknowledge that the Transition Towns movement achieved such success due to its fundamental basis in communities that want to take action for and by themselves, with an eye to wider social impacts and global concerns. *Edgeryders* might be seen as a similar community with the potential to achieve impacts on a comparable scale.

Perhaps more important, however, is what Edgeryders as individuals might be able to take from the "Transition" movement to support the establishment of their own community projects. Transition Towns have mobilised local communities, networking them internally (forging crucial links with local public administrations, for instance) as well as externally on a global scale,[93] in ways that not only support the development of local initiatives but also provide valuable information, support and guidance to likeminded people the world over. Edgeryders are already adept creators and navigators of networked communities; they simply require the kind of institutional support (at multiple levels) that helped the Transition Town movement progress from prototype to a transnational model of achievable community sustainability.

Prototyping projects or scenarios has another major advantage. Sometimes there are several possible solutions to a particular problem, with no clear consensus on how to proceed. A trial and error situation ensues, with many small-scale experiments carried out. There is much imitation, adaptation and mutation of ideas, particularly when those ideas are developed and tried out in the open space of the Internet. In essence,

---

92. James, "Practical resilience: experiments in resilience in a small UK market town", available at http://edgeryders.ppa.coe.int/practical-resilience/mission_case/experiments-resilience-small-uk-market-town, accessed 22 July 2013.
93. Transition Towns can now be found all over the world, in the US, Canada, South Africa, Australia, New Zealand, and across Europe.

there are considerable opportunities to share the outcomes of prototypes – stories of success and failure – in order to help develop solutions more efficiently. While the Internet provides the arena for these exchanges, what tends to be the barrier to more frequent sharing of problems, trials and failures is the need to succeed in order to secure progress or, often, a personal livelihood. There is often a lack of time to solve problems and experiment further. Failure is rarely a passport to an immediate income, yet this does not negate the fact that once-failed initiatives can still harbour the potential for future success, if they are worked on a little more. This is an important issue to be borne in mind by institutions when considering the nature of support to be provided to innovative projects.

Institutional support

So what support do Edgeryders need most in order to help them "make things happen"? It is clear that in many ways they are already making considerable achievements; the point is, however, that institutional support could help them scale up their projects significantly, increasing their reach and impact. And since Edgeryders projects tend to be focused on filling current policy gaps, providing support to existing initiatives may offer institutions a relatively low-cost and low-effort means of addressing them. There are two key ways in which institutions could act to help Edgeryders here.

The first concerns freeing citizens from regulations that at present constrain, even criminalise, some of their actions. A prime example would be granting easier access to unused public buildings; another would be promoting and supporting more flexible ways of learning that redefine what it means to be "qualified" to engage in particular forms of work. Allowing citizens greater scope to self-organise and self-manage means that citizens and institutions together can be far more dynamic than any institution alone in managing a whole raft of socio-economic challenges.

The second way in which institutions could help Edgeryders is in the form of direct project support. To some extent this is a matter of funding. Alberto Cottica suggests: "People – especially young people – want to save the world anyway, and if they know their bills are paid a lot more of them will give it a go."[94]

One suggestion made within *Edgeryders* is that of a guaranteed basic minimum wage for those working on community projects. This would not only negate the threat of being forced to give up community work for paid work, but it would also acknowledge

---

94. Comment by Alberto Cottica in a mission report by Edwin, "Mo money, mo problems", available at http://edgeryders.ppa.coe.int/quest-paid-work/mission_case/mo-money-mo-problems, accessed 22 July 2013.

the value of that work by pricing it. However, money is not everything to Edgeryders. Other support is needed too; particularly mechanisms that can help them scale up their projects or continue refinement and experimentation when prototypes fail. Edgeryder James talked about his UK-based initiative, Access Space, which makes use of unwanted ICT equipment by using it in information technology classes for marginalised social groups. Despite having a proven methodology with results to show, the only way Access Space was able to access European grants was to work under a regional development organisation which shielded them from a "frightening" level of bureaucracy. James writes:

> There was no way we could have accessed ERDF[95] funding with our levels of experience. We came in as a minor delivery partner, insulated from the frightening bureaucracy of the project by more experienced lead partners.[96]

Making grant access and other sorts of funding easier would undoubtedly be welcomed by Edgeryders (see the "Dear Funders" letter, Appendix B). But there remains considerable scope for policy makers to think innovatively about how they can help Edgeryders, or indeed any individual or community group (as well as themselves as policy delivery agents), in making the process of scaling up successful projects more efficient.

3.3. Building trust

The lack of faith in institutions which Edgeryders share is largely the result of the perception that institutional actions often undermine their own aims, either by failing to act on opportunities to live up to policy promises, or through policies which simply contradict one another. The result is a fundamental lack of trust amongst young people in established ways of doing politics. This does not necessarily mean that institutions themselves are distrusted (although that is not uncommon), but that they and the dominant political structures they are part of are viewed as ill-equipped to face new political challenges, utilise new participatory opportunities or adapt to new circumstances.

Furthermore, these frustrations extend to organisations that, in some respects, position themselves directly as facilitators of communication between citizens and government, such as NGOs and other third sector entities. When partnerships with these kinds of organisations are required to fulfil funders' requirements, unnecessary administrative barriers may arise, with third parties abusing their administrative power and

---

95. European Regional Development Fund.
96. James, "Access Space: a new model for individual and community development", available at http://edgeryders.ppa.coe.int/spotlight-social-innovation/mission_case/access-space-new-model-individual-and-community-development, accessed 22 July 2013.

undermining the project initiator's ability to deliver a successful project. How, then, can institutions – public, private and third sector – go about building trust such that the citizens who seek to work with them can believe that their work will be respected, supported and developed?

Clarity, transparency, reflexivity

One major problem requiring urgent resolution is that of different levels or areas of government setting policies that fail to join up. Edgeryders have found themselves trapped between policies that make competing, often contradictory demands. In one sense this is an internal communication exercise for government departments (across all levels) and policy advice bodies. But in the short term, what should citizens do when they are caught between policies? At the very least they should be assured that they will not face negative repercussions (termination of welfare support, for example). What is missing is a space for those who devise and implement conflicting policies to negotiate resolutions. At present, Edgeryders are acutely aware that governments are incapable of solving – sometimes even noticing – their own internal contradictions. Yet resolution at this level is a fundamental part of building citizens' trust in the ability of institutions to deliver on their stated aims. Policy makers need to innovate here, devising their own hacks and bridges to address these problems.

In order to do this, policy makers must get closer to the lived impacts of their policies. This tends to be a significant gap in policy development, since current institutional cultures – the norms that are followed when formulating policy – hinder, and even prevent, policy makers from interacting personally with the complexities of their policies as they play out in real life. The benefits of institutions relaxing self-written rules governing policy formulation are potentially profound, in terms of devising policies that work alongside rather than against each other. Policy makers should feel that direct engagement with the people their policies will affect is a legitimate, vital policy research tool. Rather than being condemned for attempting to push new ways of developing policies that clash with institutional politics or norms, such reaching out should be welcomed. As one policy maker who attended the Living on the Edge conference said to the assembled Edgeryders: "I need people like you to shake me up." Those who step into their constituents' world will inevitably encounter complex scenarios requiring flexible, dynamic and responsive policy instruments. However, putting these instruments in place need not, in itself, be a complex exercise, since Edgeryders often seek less rather than more direct institutional involvement. What they need is for institutions to be allies rather than enforcers.

Allies rather than enforcers

Edgeryders were clear about the need for allies of all sorts during the transition to an independent life. While they acknowledged family, friends and peers as valuable allies in providing forms of assistance ranging from food and a place to live to moral support and seed funding, they were equally clear about the difficulties of forming allegiances with institutions. Alberto Cottica, for instance, expressed his frustration at the dismissal of a successful social policy prototype he designed (at taxpayers' expense) when changes in government meant that projects associated with the previous administration were scrapped.[97] SimoneMuffolini relayed the story of his efforts to implement a rural local development plan that was obstructed and denied support from government institutions at several different levels.[98] Similar stories of Edgeryders' actions being blocked or simply ignored by the institutions with whom they wanted to work were remarkably common, yet opening up to the initiatives presented to them may in fact have offered those institutions solutions to social problems that they had otherwise been unable to solve, or even address. In this respect, Edgeryders and institutions could quite easily fulfil some of each other's needs; this would simply require institutions to stop thinking of themselves as enforcers of rules and inhibitors of actions, and reposition themselves as allies in bringing about positive change.

Institutions could be better allies merely by granting Edgeryders more space. There are two senses in which this is the case. The first concerns Edgeryders' projects or initiatives. These require a period in which Edgeryders and their collaborators are simply left to get on with it. If the project is strong enough, there may be a case for providing institutional support to help that project develop, grow, or otherwise become sustainable. Edgeryder Alessia Zabatino, talking about her work in bringing unused public buildings back into use, writes:

> In this case I mean that before deciding to evict a space the Administration should give time for the project to evolve, if a project has been clearly presented. The Administration should observe how the district and the whole city react and it should dialogue with the occupants because they are the most direct interlocutors, they are the problem that is looking for a solution.[99]

97. Comment by Alberto in a mission report by Beckery, "Small scale vs large scale efficiency", available at http://edgeryders.ppa.coe.int/making-sense-edgeryders-experiences-where-do-we-go-here/mission_case/help-handbook-please-small-scal#comment-4047, accessed 22 July 2013.
98. Comment by Alberto, ibid.
99. Alessia Zabatino, "The acknowledgement of social value: the legitimate illegality culture as a commons. A journey through the Italian spaces occupied by knowledge workers" #2, available at http://edgeryders.ppa.coe.int/protecting-and-enhancing-commons/mission_case/legitimate-illegality-culture-commons-journey-through-, accessed 22 July 2013.

Before a project has reached the stage at which it can be evaluated as a "prototype", those behind it need support – or, at least, tolerance – from the local authorities. This is not to say that authorities should turn a blind eye to citizens' activities until it suits them; rather that there may be, for instance, a strong case for relaxing legislation that might otherwise inhibit the development of the project. Communication between citizens and institutions forms a fundamental part of ensuring this can be achieved, and being open to these kinds of conversations, as well as delivering on promises made, is a key means for institutions to be better allies. By giving citizens' projects space to flourish and by remaining engaged with project workers throughout, institutions potentially have a major role to play as facilitators of social cohesion, as well as collaborators in the reduction of waste.

The second way in which Edgeryders would benefit from being granted more space by institutions-as-allies is more personal. There was a strong sense within the *Edgeryders* community that they are expected to hurry their transition from youth to an independent life. Cultural expectations about the "right" way to go about navigating this complex part of the life course, or what a "successful" transition looks like, have been formalised in policies that add more pressure to achieve stability in a socio-economic context where doing so is increasingly difficult. Since there is no longer any guarantee of a secure career in almost any field of work, Edgeryders need the opportunity to experiment and explore, find out what their skills are and discover talents or interests they did not know they had, get feedback and input from peers, and learn for themselves where and how they can best contribute to bringing some form of stability back into their lives. In essence, more than any generation before them, Edgeryders need the space to learn how to become resilient. Confidence and self-efficacy come from having tried things and taken risks, but institutions often view what may appear to be a prolonged period of experimentation with suspicion. There is a clear link here with the challenges associated with portfolio careers, discussed above. In both realms there is a pressing need for widespread change in cultural norms and expectations. The private sector in particular has a key role to play in normalising acceptance in the professional sphere of transitions comprised of diverse – but demonstrably valuable – experiences. But there is far more to the establishment of new cultural norms that policy makers must become aware of.

3.4. New cultural norms

A raft of unrealistic expectations based on socio-cultural norms with fading relevance has proved to be a source of significant anxiety for many Edgeryders. Most commonly these have concerned topics such as career paths, educational choices and job models, but they also extend to issues such as having a family. Existing norms about how to navigate a "successful" transition to an independent life are counterproductive, since the socio-economic landscape has changed fundamentally and the resources to which Edgeryders have access are different. While expectations are perpetuated throughout every realm of everyday life – through family, peers, colleagues, global media – institutions have a key role in creating and validating those expectations through the ways in which everyday life is directed through policy.

Edgeryder IdilM's concern about unpaid internships is a good example.[100] Here the absence of a clear policy stance on fair payments for interns has allowed institutions to keep their own costs low at a high personal cost to young people seeking work experience. The acceptance of unpaid internships as a norm has been founded on the ability of more privileged young people to obtain familial financial support, yet such support is available to fewer and fewer young people as the economic crisis hits family finances hard. An urgent cultural shift is therefore required in which institutions reframe their expectations about young people's needs and resources based on their current precarious circumstances. A key part of this will be constructing new definitions of the multiple ways in which young people create value, as discussed above.

What may in fact be required is a whole new vocabulary for the articulation of young people's transitions. Alessia Zabatino talks about having developed a new vocabulary in the process of navigating her own transition, "in which 'occupy' means 'taking care' and 'commons' are places for the construction of other economies and pure forms of co-operation and sociality, other forms of government, new forms of social enterprises".[101]

This is a strong reflection of the fact that, for Edgeryders, the ways in which they spend their time constitute their mode of voting for what they believe is important and what they want their institutions to support. It is clear that, for young people, political participation now takes a much wider range of forms than voting in elections, and that often it blurs into other areas of life, such as making a living or community involvement (Eriksson 2012).

If Edgeryders must make sense of their transitions by reframing the ways in which they describe their experiences, policies, too, must reflect this shift by updating their own vocabularies to accommodate these new meanings, as well as by creating an enabling

---

100. IdilM, "The quest for paid work: unpaid internships are discriminatory and should be ended", available at http://edgeryders.ppa.coe.int/quest-paid-work/mission_case/unpaid-internships-are-discriminatory-and-should-be-ended-0, accessed 22 July 2013.

101. Alessia Zabatino, "The acknowledgement of social value: the legitimate illegality culture as a commons. A journey through the Italian spaces occupied by knowledge workers" #2, available at http:// edgeryders.ppa.coe.int/protecting-and-enhancing-commons/mission_case/legitimate-illegality-culture-commons-journey-through-, accessed 22 July 2013.

environment in which they can be lived in practice. Not only would this facilitate better understanding, better support, and stronger mutual trust, it presents an opportunity to bridge an intergenerational gulf which, at present, is a key factor in maintaining counterproductive, outdated cultural norms. The Edgeryders' generation has embraced a paradigm of social innovation, as well as new ways of being political, which older generations find difficult to understand. Leadership from institutions that speak the same language, literally, as that used by young people can infiltrate the everyday understandings of the wider population as new norms are established.

Creating and embedding new norms is not, and can never be, the responsibility of a single group. However, the responsibility for beginning the process should lie with those facing the most significant risks if those new norms fail to take root. Edgeryders are already taking significant risks in order to carve out a new culture – pushing new forms of learning, working, living together – that still remains marginal to European cultures at large. But governments, too, face significant risks if they fail to keep pace with the ways in which contemporary young people's transitions foretell the changing shape of education, labour markets, politics and economies.

The priority of most governments is a contented, employed, prosperous population, not one that is frustrated, disaffected and impoverished (not only financially). The economic impacts of a sense of insecurity are considerable – as the vulnerability of European economies continues to reveal. Part of the solution, at least in terms of the place of youth within the bigger picture, is for institutions, especially governments, to validate the ways in which young people are making sense of their place in a complex world. This can be done by providing the kind of support that acknowledges them as valued and valuable experiences. At present, institutions appear content to play a key part in producing the challenging youth transition landscape, but less able to accept its results – young people with a multiplicity of skills but no single, natural "slot" in society. There is, as a result, a pressing need for positive reinforcement of the new kinds of working life which Edgeryders' experiences constitute. As Edgeryder Ben suggests:

> Whilst it is true that this generation is unlikely to be as economically prosperous as their parents' generation, this isn't necessarily reflective of a lack of productivity and creativity but rather a lack of visibility of how recent graduates have continued to work during recession.[102]

102. Ben Vickers, "Professional reality development", available at http://edgeryders.ppa.coe.int/spotlight-social-innovation/mission_case/professional-reality-development, accessed 22 July 2013.

Living on the edge ... and moving forward?

A post on the *Edgeryders* project blog from June 2012 reads:

> We have so much creative freedom, so much scope to respond to our crises beyond the simple models of elections and parties, all the way through to new economies, Wikipedia-type collaboration, changing cultures and changing goals. The future is wide open, and we hope to reach as far into it as possible, and lay the foundations for making it real at the European level.[103]

Edgeryders' experiences as presented here demonstrate two crucial things. First, young people are responding to the challenges they face in negotiating their transitions in a hugely difficult socio-economic context by taking action on their own terms. In other words, existing norms, systems and policies are less and less relevant to their needs, as a result of which they are formulating their own norms and systems, and articulating them with a new vocabulary. The second point concerns the urgency with which institutions must respond by recasting the ways in which they make policy, as well as the policies themselves, in order to reflect the nature of contemporary youth transitions and provide the support mechanisms that European youth need.

What we have seen on *Edgeryders* is how contemporary youth are active in creating their own initiatives and spaces, which work with different kinds of practices than those which characterise institutional politics. The question is, can institutions redefine their role as sources of information, guidance and support rather than as orchestrators of forms of political participation that, for today's young people, serve little meaningful purpose?

The next section is a call to action which draws on Edgeryders' own suggestions as to how policies and institutions might more effectively and efficiently support the needs of their young constituents.

4. Call to action

As a project, *Edgeryders* represents an experimental space to articulate the real-life experiences of European youth. The platform has clearly demonstrated that European youth are engaging in active citizenship based on self-formulated procedures and practices fundamentally different from those employed in conventional institutional politics and policy delivery. Those participating have, in developing new modes of political participation and social action, pointed to the necessity of new forms of policy research, development and delivery. What role, then, should be taken by institutions to

---

103. Blog post by Edgeryder Vinay, "At the beginning of the end, or the beginning of a new Europe?", available at http://cookiesncode.wordpress.com/2012/06/04/at-the-beginning-of-the-end-or-the-beginning-of-a-new-europe, accessed 22 July 2013.

support these most effectively? This chapter presents some ways of moving forward in the immediate future, building directly on the activities of Edgeryders.

4.1. Champion new cultural norms

Of paramount importance is political championship of new cultural norms, particularly those that redefine accepted ways of learning and working, in response to the emergent needs of young people and the societies in which they live. This is about embedding diversity and flexibility within the cultural mindset through norms that better reflect the nature of young people's transitions, accommodate their abilities and needs, and respond to the present socio-economic situation, particularly the persistence (even growth, in some areas) of social inequalities. Focusing on working and learning in order to reflect Edgeryders' widely shared concerns about having the "right" skills and knowledge for their transitions, policy makers could consider the mechanisms described below.

Flexicurity and transitional labour markets

Flexicurity and transitional labour markets are concerned with accommodating multiple forms of work whilst reducing precariousness (van Lieshout and Wilthagen 2003). They are premised on permeable labour markets which allow individuals to combine different forms of employment, including paid and non-paid work (volunteering), and multiple income sources, such as wages and state benefits. Transitional labour markets are particularly able to support transitions between part-time and full-time employment, including circumstances where an individual is studying part-time for additional qualifications, or moving from salaried work to self-employment (or vice versa). Further, they incorporate legally enforceable entitlements for young people to choose from different employment options according to their needs, while fiscal incentives encourage employment rather than state-financed unemployment. These principles mean various transition pathways are possible, with young people able to switch between them depending on their changing needs. Flexicurity should provide a basic income for young people in transition who are confronted with the insecurities of flexi-jobs and who are denied working contracts (Stauber et al. 2003).

These mechanisms, which the Netherlands and Denmark have already experimented with, have a potentially significant role to play in integrating and, importantly, culturally validating diverse transition constellations. By reducing the personal risk associated with acquiring a diverse skill set from multiple contexts, they facilitate entry to the (necessarily more dynamic) labour market by permitting a range of alternative routes. For Edgeryders concerned with the impact of their "portfolio" careers on their ability to achieve stability, these approaches offer both a degree of security and the flexibility to continue developing their skills and experience. And for those like Edgeryder Edwin's friend, forced to choose between meaningful unpaid work and meaningless paid employment, they offer a means of reconciliation.

This is also the context in which to redress the issue of the undervaluing (in monetary terms) of young people's work. A labour market attitude that expects young people to work for free, contributing to an organisation at their own cost (to draw on the example of unpaid internships), simply has no place in a context where transitional labour markets and flexicurity are established norms. Transnational institutions, widely viewed as popular internship destinations, have a leading role to play in counteracting the failure to recognise young people's work through monetary recompense, through their own practice as much as through any policies that might be set. Doing so would not only contribute to a more widespread re-evaluation of young people's work and provide them with the recognition and security they have the right to expect, it would also express clear institutional commitment to "walking the talk" of addressing social inequalities.

Learning communities

It was painfully clear from Edgeryders' stories that, in their experience, formal education (particularly the formal components such as secondary school) is oppressive, inflexible and fails to provide the requisite knowledge to support their transitions in the "real world". Beyond the apparent inability of formal education to equip young people for independent life, the continued emphasis in policy development and educational institutions on education rather than learning has significant implications for social mobility which need to be addressed (Gutiérrez-Esteban and Mikiewicz 2012). Essentially, the field of learning opportunities needs both levelling, in order to increase access to learning opportunities for those marginalised by mainstream forms of education, and widening, in order to legitimise a much more diverse range of learning opportunities.

This is all the more important since, as Edgeryders have demonstrated, dense social networks are increasingly a key means of gaining social capital (that is, knowledge, information and skills) and it is important that these networks are open to all who want to participate and contribute. The pursuit of social capital has been theorised as a quest for lost community (Coleman 1991; Putnam 2001) and there is vivid evidence of this sentiment within the *Edgeryders* community. As a means of tackling social inequalities and opening up access to social capital, policy should move towards a view of learning as a multi-faceted, multi-method process, and in recognition of this, reframe formal education in terms of dynamic learning communities. In these contexts the valourisation of collaborative working is implicit and the value of informal learning spaces is acknowledged. Edgeryder Brightfutureforall described what this might look like in practice:

> Schools could play an important role, working closely with local associations they can better direct students [to] opportunities in line with their interests, creating a more active community and giving kids a chance to prove themselves, feel passionate about a cause or help people in need. Incentives should be put into place to encourage students to take up these opportunities, also building on programs already into place, giving preferential treatment to students that enriched their education through languages and volunteer experiences.[104]

If, as the European Commission states, Europe's youth needs to be equipped to take advantage of opportunities such as civic and political participation, volunteering, creativity and entrepreneurship (European Commission 2009), they must have access to learning opportunities to help them do so. Since the consensus amongst Edgeryders is that present systems are failing to deliver these opportunities, the system must be recalibrated by incorporating a wider range of components. As Edgeryders have demonstrated, the Internet has opened up access to a vast array of educational resources which independent learners of all sorts are already making use of. This should force the hand of institutions which have remained wedded to education as it is traditionally defined; they themselves have the opportunity to learn from the examples of independent learners which are the most effective, engaging and, from a transferable skills point of view, useful techniques. Embracing these well-established, if still disparate, forms of learning will have multiple positive impacts: young people will be better able to acquire the skills they need to be flexible and resilient members of the labour market; social inequalities will be reduced as a result of the opening up of access to social capital; and a new culture of learning will be mapped out based on community and collaboration, which is a much closer match to the emerging demands of the labour market.

Beyond these forms of "personal" learning for Edgeryders' own futures, there is an additional need for (physical and/or virtual) spaces in which citizens and institutional representatives can learn, solve problems and collaborate on an equal footing. These spaces should provide opportunities for citizens to increase their understanding of governance structures and policy architectures and processes. At the same time they have the potential to offer valuable opportunities for policy makers to gain awareness of the lived realities of current policies. Most importantly, however, they should exist to facilitate citizen participation in the design of new policy instruments characterised by creative responses to the most pressing social challenges. A fundamental part of this

---

104. Brightfutureforall, "Reality check: opportunities", available at http://edgeryders.ppa.coe.int/reality-check/mission_case/opportunities, accessed 22 July 2013.

process should be the collective attempt to make sense of these challenges by citizens and institutional representatives, as well as the joint presentation of potential solutions for democratic debate. A process of this kind would result in collaboratively mapped-out policies and delivery methods, as well as better mutual understanding of each party's needs and constraints, thus maximising the chances of successful outcomes.

4.2. Redesign policy-making processes

It is not just that policies concerned with youth require reframing in light of the changing nature of their transitions. The ways in which policy is made also require urgent attention. Communication technologies, particularly the Internet, have made it easier than ever before for citizens to observe and comment on how policies are designed, communicated and delivered. It is no longer the case that citizens have to leave power in the hands of elected (or unelected) officials for the duration of their administrations. Edgeryder Carlien Roodink is confident that "we can do better than that".[105] Yet, as things stand at present, youth policy tends to focus on fostering participation in decisions within areas that are already defined as influencing the lives of young people. The problem, however, is often not (only) that the wrong decisions are being made, but that there is no policy working on the issues that young people consider most important (Eriksson 2012). The young people active on *Edgeryders* would hardly settle for participation in a consultation exercise where the problem has already been defined.

In light of commitments at the European level to involve young people in the formulation of youth policies and elicit their views about their effectiveness once implemented (Council of Europe 2008; Denstad 2009), it is essential that institutions deliver on these intentions. This is not only because of the greater transparency afforded by the Internet, but also because consultation increases the likelihood of policies being implemented effectively and experienced positively. This means more than simply finding new ways of asking questions or measuring outcomes. The aim of redesigning policy-making processes should be to have a positive direct impact on the ways in which participation, citizenship, access to commons, and so on are valued by society. In other words, they should build trust among citizens that institutions understand the everyday realities they face. The following part outlines some of the ways they might go about this.

---

105. Carlien Roodink, comment on a mission report by Alessia Zabatino, "The acknowledgement of social value: the legitimate illegality culture as a commons. A journey through the Italian spaces occupied by knowledge workers #2", available at http://edgeryders.ppa.coe.int/protecting-and-enhancing-commons/mission_case/legitimate-illegality-culture-commons-journey-through-, accessed 22 July 2013.

Engage with young people in their own spaces

In order to obtain an accurate picture of how youth policy is experienced "on the ground", policy makers need to engage with young people in the context of their lived realities, rather than creating specifically designed policy consultation spaces, which, for young people already sceptical about institutional attempts at consultation, seem like little more than a box-ticking exercise. As has been noted, "inserting one or a few youth into an adult-created and adult-driven process runs the risk of involving youth as tokens or 'decorations'" (O'Donoghue et al. 2003), and "simply participating in a process that is already defined does not guarantee real influence" (Eriksson 2012). However, if policy makers are genuinely keen to put expertise and evidence at the heart of policy-making processes, the greatest experts are youth and the most compelling evidence is to be found in their everyday lives. This is where policy makers need to spend much more time.

It is clear from the frustrations articulated by Edgeryders that institutions are, at present, not as capable as they should be with regards to taking charge of the process of participation. Indeed, they are currently less capable than young people themselves could be. Compared with the forms of communication and organisation that Edgeryders and their peers wield so effectively, institutional processes are slow and rarely given to experimentation. However, once institutions turn to action they are capable of impact on the sort of scale that small grassroots initiatives often find unmanageable. The key question, then, is how to join up the spaces in which young people are already active with those of the policy domain, via channels through which real influence can be exerted. Even during natural lulls in the policy-making process, continually observing how policies are experienced in citizens' everyday lives potentially offers revealing insights useful for future policy iterations. A comment from Edgeryder Neal Gorenflo, for instance, illustrates how observing the ways in which citizens live out relatively mundane aspects of their lives – such as the modes of transport they choose – can be vital signposts:

> And second, the time you free up by sharing and living more simply can be used to get engaged in issues that affect your lifestyle. For instance, going car-free is a lot easier if there's plenty of bike lanes and good public transportation. These are community issues that you can't work toward alone. You have to get involved in your community to make sure your tax dollars are spent in ways that make simpler living possible.[106]

Yet exactly how to join up citizens' spaces with the policy sphere requires careful thought since at present, each party remains wary of the motives of the other.

---

106. Neal Gorenflo, "Share your ryde: interview with a sharer", available at http://edgeryders.ppa.coe. int/share-your-ryde/mission_case/interview-sharer, accessed 22 July 2013.

Furthermore, involving the kinds of organisations which are in a position to function as intermediaries (such as NGOs) is not without its own set of challenges. There is little incentive, for instance, for an NGO to promote novel, low-cost solutions it cannot take credit for.

On the other hand, an appropriate and mutually accessibly online space has the potential to reach people far out in the frequency distribution of any given citizenry, including those who would not ordinarily seek out opportunities to express views on politics or civil affairs. All signs from *Edgeryders* point to this being the space in which these exchanges should happen. However, it is clear that there is still some discomfort within government institutions about how to respond to them. Edgeryder Carlien Roodink, who straddles the Edgeryder-institution divide, writes:

> Politicians (I am a member of the city council of Amsterdam) and government are used to cooperat[ing] with legal entities which are easy to define. For example: we know who the members of the board are of a foundation. In the case of a labor union we know the number of registered and paying members. Social networks and online communities can be far more vital and effective than those old organizations but are less clear to define.[107]

The boundaries of online communities may be far more blurred than those institutions are used to dealing with, inevitably making them harder to manage, but this is a challenge institutions must grapple with, since online networks are only going to become more powerful. Working out how best to make use of these spaces is only the first part of the process, however. An essential part of closing the communications gap between institutions and citizens involves visibly making use of the data gathered. Not only will this fulfil any commitments made to evidence-based policy, it will reassure citizens that the contributions they make to policy processes are valued, thus establishing a relationship between citizens and institutions based on confidence and trust – which, to date, has been sorely lacking.

Design and deliver "Policy 2.0"

Articulating his perception that young people are blocked from participating more fully in policy processes by institutions' lack of knowledge of new media instruments, Edgeryder Emiliano Fatello suggests that policy makers "don't know Policy 2.0."[108] In essence, they have failed to keep pace with the ways in which decision making has

---

107. Comment by Carlien Roodink in a mission report by Demsoc, "Networking the networks", available at http://edgeryders.ppa.coe.int/reactivating-democratic-institutions/mission_case/networking-networks, accessed 22 July 2013.
108. Emiliano Fatello, "Live not survive", available at http:/ /edgeryders.ppa.coe.int/bootcamp/mission_case/live-not-survive, accessed 22 July 2013.

evolved to incorporate new technologies. At least, this is the way institutions appear to young people. This sense was widely shared in the Edgeryder community. Cataspanglish relayed the experiences of several Edgeryders through a series of interviews, revealing the view of one of his subjects, Anne, that:

> most of the policy makers and institutions are really far away from understanding the experience of people who have grown up with the Internet as a normal part of their lives.[109]

Ben, similarly, saw this as being a significant barrier to forging a more productive relationship between institutions and citizens:

> we'd like to create positive change but as it currently stands the jobs, institutions and organisations available to us do not appear to have the frameworks or courage to instigate that change and until they do we're unlikely to build any meaningful allegiances.[110]

In one sense, then, using the full range of available technologies in order to engage young people in their (online) spaces is a fundamental part of moving towards "Policy 2.0". An equally important part, however, is how these tools are used to address knowledge silos within the policy-making process. The social policy landscape at present is beset by many complex, interlinked challenges – and not only those that directly concern youth. Managing these requires dynamism across departmental or portfolio responsibilities, and, at times, the jurisdictional boundaries of government. Uniting collective intelligence and expertise from separate but interlinked agencies, policy domains and jurisdictional areas is likely to better enable effective responses to the most complex of social policy challenges.

The growth of open data has started to facilitate this. The more information is publicly shared among government departments and other policy institutions, the easier it is to identify not only how young people respond to one particular policy, but also how they respond to others which are concerned with similar or interrelated issues. Furthermore, combining this with the open source approach to collaborative problem solving presents a potentially low-cost, low-resource means of canvassing opinion on topics that cut across government departments. Edgeryder JOYE presented a case on the project platform that constitutes a good example of how this might work:

> perhaps the next time that the town council is deciding on the layout and location of a children's play-area, they could source their ideas directly from the public by allowing a

---

109. Cataspanglish, "The quest for paid work: (making a) living on the edge: Anne Wizorek", available at http:// edgeryders.ppa.coe.int/quest-paid-work/mission_case/making-living-edge-anne-wizorek, accessed 22 July 2013.
110. Ben Vickers, "The quest for paid work: post art school hinterland: earning in the grey zones of the artworld", available at http://edgeryders.ppa.coe.int/quest-paid-work/mission_case/post-art-school-hinterland-earning-grey-zones-artworld, accessed 22 July 2013.

web-accessible location where people could actively contribute to the design and development of that area – not just through allowing comment, but allowing actual direct collaboration? An online blueprint with an interface that allows annotation, or from which items can be removed, added, upvoted or downvoted?[111]

In this scenario, citizens respond to information provided by a local authority (open data) by offering their own suggestions on a policy issue (open sourcing solutions), which in turn are then subject to comment and discussion involving all stakeholders (a combination of open data and open source solutions). Not only does this involve the community in formulating decisions that best suit their needs, it makes the process of translating discussions into a workable policy visible to citizens – including, importantly, communicating those elements which for reasons of budget, safety or current legislation are simply not possible. Limited resources at local administration level mean that citizens need to reach consensus on their priorities and aggregate their efforts prior to engaging in a collaborative policy planning exercise. This was recognised by Edgeryder Stefano in his mission report on participatory budgeting:

> The democratic mechanism is quite simple: citizens formulate proposals, public servants evaluate them and citizens vote the priorities, those who must be realized right now. They must be aware of simple rules: the more they are, the more they get. That is to say, they should make the effort to gather and come up with a joint or common project which is much more likely to find widespread support from the bottom up. In this sense, being aware of the economic restraints (the budget) is a valid incentive to realize that we are part a world of limited resources and nobody can pretend to get simply what they want.[112]

Since these kinds of collaborative efforts are well placed to save local administrations both time and money, as well as help them develop policies to which citizens are likely to be far more receptive, there is a strong case for investing in a framework which guides citizens through this process. However, any institution doing so would need to bear in mind the points discussed above – the need to use the right tools in the right spaces, and the need for the process to be collaborative rather than merely consultative. For young people, in particular, who have much to gain as well as much to offer in these processes, the opportunity to be part of shaping support mechanisms that can ease the transition to an independent life cannot come too quickly.

---

111. JOYE, "We, the sharers: the town as an open source project", available at http://edgeryders.ppa.coe. int/we-sharers/mission_case/town-open-source-project, accessed 22 July 2013.
112. Stefano, "Reactivating democratic institutions: participatory budgeting worldwide!", available at http://edgeryders.ppa.coe.int/reactivating-democratic-institutions/mission_case/participatory-budgeting-worldwide, accessed 22 July 2013.

4.3. Provide more timely support mechanisms

Many Edgeryders who have set up (or attempted to set up) their own enterprises have been frustrated by the difficulty of securing the right kind of institutional support at the right time. Open-ended, networked and process-oriented participation is extremely effective in getting projects started, gathering people, spreading information and generating energy. But after the initial phase, consolidating those first achievements can be more difficult. It is at this stage that institutional support is most needed. In other words, institutional support is needed for project maintenance and sustainability, rather than generating the first flurries of activity (although it is important to note that some kinds of projects would benefit from support here too, particularly in the form of accessible seed funding). However, there is a current imbalance between funding structures that privilege short-term contracts and interventions that require long-term commitments to achieve the desired impact (Eriksson 2012). Many projects involve numerous stakeholders in a promising effort but when the funding is exhausted and the project is forced to wind down, the situation reverts to what it was before the intervention, with little change having been actually achieved.

What is needed at this point is help in scaling up successful initiatives. Ultimately, governments want policies and delivery mechanisms that produce big impacts. But, certainly for Edgeryders, they are most engaged in tackling problems for themselves and their immediate communities – in other words, localised issues – in large part because acting at this scale is difficult enough when there are few resources at hand. This is not to say, however, that their solutions could not be transferred or scaled up with the right support. It takes institutional resources and political power to achieve this.

There are two ways in which this could happen; which method is most suitable depends very much on the nature of the initiative. The first method involves providing resources (financial, infrastructural, political, and so on) in a specific locale in order to grow the project, increasing its reach to larger numbers of people. This approach would be best suited to an initiative such as Access Space, an open digital arts lab in the UK which provides ICT workshops and drop-in sessions for local people with low incomes.[113] The second method is better suited to projects the purpose of which is not to scale up but to multiply. Here, impact is achieved when enough people are involved in many small-scale, local initiatives. What remains a problem in this instance is the workload of co-ordination, something that a larger actor with more resources is better able to handle, since then every entity (that is, each local chapter of a project) does not have to communicate with each other, only with a central point of contact. A key role for

---

113. www.access-space.org/doku.php, accessed 22 July 2013.

institutions in these contexts, then, is one of connectors or aggregators – much like the Edgeryder-initiated project "We live here", which aims to "create a civic space by networking the networks that already exist in the community."[114]

While acknowledging that the administrative costs of providing support for many small initiatives can be seen as prohibitively high, there is nevertheless a pressing need to introduce appropriate administrative processes that remove some of the obstacles to providing institutional support to smaller initiatives. Some members of the *Edgeryders* community are already in the early stages of devising an international bridging inter-face between funders and local, small initiatives.[115] This presents a ripe opportunity for institutions.

4.4. Take some risks!

Ethnographical analysis of the data gathered through the *Edgeryders* project reveals that Edgeryders, as well as their families, tend to bear all the risk in their attempts to transition to an independent life. Making best guesses about the "right" education and career choices, moving from city to city in pursuit of better opportunities, and bearing the financial risks associated with this instability mean that young people often remain dependent on the financial and emotional support of family or close friends, rather than achieving independence. Yet such is the depth of the economic crisis in Europe that it is reasonable to ask how long it will be possible to assume families can shoulder the added burden of supporting their adult children.

The imbalance in the burden of risk in contemporary young Europeans' transitions reflects a glaring absence of institutional leadership, which, so far, has provided little in the way of formal policy safety nets (such as guaranteed wages for community work) or culturally validated alternative transition pathways. It is time for institutions to relieve young people of some of the risks they face by taking them on and dispersing them at an institutional level. The rewards that could be reaped are significant – more young people being economically active means lower welfare payments and much-needed economic, civic and political stimulus.

An essential part of this rebalancing of risk depends on institutions absolving young people's families of at least some of the financial responsibility for supporting their

---

114. Demsoc, "Networking the networks", available at http://edgeryders.ppa.coe.int/reactivating-democratic-institutions/mission_case/networking-networks, accessed 22 July 2013.
115. The conversation is posted in a mission report by Darren, "Where Edgeryders dare: can we and should we pull off an official Edgeryders organisation?", available at http://edgeryders.ppa.coe.int/where-edgeryders-dare/mission_case/can-we-and-should-we-pull-official-edgeryders-organisation, accessed 22 July 2013.

transitions. Funding for innovation and entrepreneurialism is an important component of this, as is valuing in monetary terms the work young people do to contribute to community well-being, sustainability and cohesion. Some of the topics discussed by Edgeryders could have a role here as "wildcard" forms of financial support and economic stimulus: crowdfunding, crowdmatching, angel investors, basic income, barter currencies and time banking. These support systems must be visible and accessible in order to encourage innovation and active citizenship amongst a wider range of young people, and to ensure that engaging in these activities is an active choice because they know the support is there, rather than an act of desperation or frustration in the face of few other opportunities. One relatively low-resource solution here would be to use publicly funded websites as a communication infrastructure to support citizen initiatives. This kind of knowledge hub would be particularly beneficial to those projects for which gathering public support is fundamental to their reaching critical mass. Furthermore, it would help institutions to achieve widespread positive local impacts by supporting community efforts to help themselves, at low cost and effort.

However, taking risks on supporting young people's transitions is not simply about financial investment, or even the provision of other material resources. Beyond these, perhaps the risk that Edgeryders would most appreciate institutions taking lies in trusting the ways in which young people perceive and act in the world. Edgeryders want institutions to understand that the ways in which young people are going about navigating the transition to an independent life have manifold benefits at all levels of society, but that for these benefits to have their greatest impact requires young people as their instigators to be given the space, trust and resources to demonstrate their potential. It is clear from the profound difficulties faced by contemporary youth in Europe, reflected in youth unemployment figures, that lack of support means wasted potential, and wasted potential means a generation whose ability to contribute economically, politically and socially is severely constrained. As Edgeryder Alberto Masetti-Zannini says:

> A little social innovation in the policy world could really change the lives of millions of people. Policy-makers: what are you waiting for to really support social innovation?[116]

Conclusions

Current EU and Council of Europe white papers, resolutions and other policy documents make clear that, at a transnational level, the importance of working with young people to formulate the policies that impact on their lives is now widely acknowledged. What is

---

116. Alberto Masetti-Zannini, "Spotlight: social innovation: who will really support social innovation?", available at http://edgeryders.ppa.coe.int/spotlight-social-innovation/mission_case/who-will-really-support-social-innovation, accessed 22 July 2013.

evident from *Edgeryders*, however, is that despite this acknowledgement, these intentions are rarely translating into policies or forms of youth engagement that connect with young people's most pressing concerns. The purpose of *Edgeryders* has been to open up a space within which frustrations can be aired and solutions proposed, while also demonstrating the value of maintaining open communication between citizens and institutions. This conclusion reflects on what *Edgeryders* as a project has suggested about future directions for youth policy; the extent to which *Edgeryders* can be described as a successful policy research mechanism; and the ways in which *Edgeryders* has fulfilled its other aims beyond informing policy.

Where next for youth policy?

Youth policies will and should, by their very nature, remain concerned with young people's transitions to independent living. What is now abundantly clear is that these transitions are more complex, variable and protracted than ever before. In order to maximise the potential for economic prosperity and social cohesion among youth and across Europe as a whole, policy institutions must respond effectively to the changing needs of young citizens. Policies concerned with youth transitions, directly or indirectly, should be judged according to the space they provide for or withhold from young people in terms of the power and resources to which they have access in their attempts to be active citizens and live independent lives. An essential part of this policy shift will be a move by institutions towards a more pluralistic approach. Pluralism allows greater dynamism, flexibility and responsiveness in the context of youth citizens whose life trajectories may shift at every turn. In essence, pluralism contributes to the socio-political validation of multiple ways of achieving transition by providing more opportunities for young people to attain success and independence.

It is not only the fragmentation and de-standardisation of youth transitions that demand a new, pluralistic policy approach. In light of the need for individual nation states to respond to their own unique circumstances while remaining engaged with shared European concerns, a transnationally sanctioned or even transnationally mandated pluralism has the potential to provide a framework, perhaps even a toolkit, from which nations can select and employ the most appropriate delivery vehicles. This is a particularly important means of driving new forms of policy delivery in national contexts, since youth policy garners more attention at transnational level than at national level in some countries. At the same time, those formulating policy must remain alert to the interrelations and interdependencies among the multiple policy areas that affect young people's lives. For example, it might not be policy on education that influences the creation of alternative learning spaces the most, but urban development, property prices or intellectual property.

The implications of globalisation, mobility, migration and democratic renewal, amongst other issues, highlight the need to constantly review the nature of youth policy, in terms of what it aims to achieve, its scope, how it is formulated and how it is delivered. This has to take place within a sophisticated understanding of the changing patterns of youth transitions and the new challenges facing young people across Europe. *Edgeryders* researcher Magnus Eriksson has suggested: "Perhaps the issues of young people are both more global and more local than the national or regional level of institutional politics." (Eriksson 2012) As such, future youth policies must acknowledge the "glocal" nature of young people's transitions through the development of appropriately plural-istic, multi-scale support mechanisms. Such mechanisms, tailored to the needs of Edgeryders as presented here, should incorporate:

— funding streams (grants and loans) specifically for initiatives that promote the pooling and sharing of resources, including (co-)housing, (co-)working spaces and (re)opening access to commons, as well as mechanisms to help successful projects scale up or spread to new locations;

— the means to aggregate and disseminate knowledge scattered across Europe which, once identified and directed appropriately, could be of significant benefit to citizen initiatives across the region (thus following the principles of open data);

— a commitment to the reduction of waste: not only wasted funds, but wasted resources (buildings, green spaces and other commons), and wasted human potential.

Edgeryders as a successful policy mechanism

It has been suggested that providing better support for young people's transitions in Europe is not simply a case of formulating new policies, but instead requires the re-negotiation of the relationship between youth and political institutions (Eriksson 2012). *Edgeryders* as a project has broken the mould here. By providing a space for discussion, collaboration and the sharing of problems over the course of a year (the project began in October 2011), and by bringing Edgeryders face to face with some of the policy makers whose actions are shaping their lives (the Living on the Edge conference in June 2012), this project has emphatically responded to EU and Council of Europe aspirations to engage in policy making which moves beyond mere con-sultation. Beyond fulfilling its own aims in this regard, *Edgeryders* is already proving extremely useful as a means of responding to direct requests from policy makers for input on youth topics. As Alberto Cottica says in a comment on Nadia's mission report, "Learning to live": "It is a strong sign that the community has been able to convey credible, even authoritative advice in a very structured policy process, so much that it has been recruited into a second one." [117]

The question to ask at this stage is: to what extent could *Edgeryders* itself be used as a prototype for new modes of citizen-focused, deliberative, democratic forms of participation? How could it be adapted to different levels of governance and different types of government? The form of participation that comprises the prototyping culture of *Edgeryders* is adapted to uncertainty, chaotic organisation, and trial and error. It is experimental in character, examines different ways of doing things and questions overarching goals. Being asked to embrace a process that, by its nature, is chaotic and experimental may discomfit institutions used to research methods characterised by low levels of risk and high levels of control. Yet, by participating in citizen-led exploratory initiatives rather than formal, institutionally determined decision-making processes, citizens such as Edgeryders learn not just how political processes are structured today, but also how they could be structured in ways that better fulfil both citizen and institutional aims and needs. In this respect, there is much for institutions to learn from collaborative research exercises such as *Edgeryders*, not only in terms of the lived impacts of policies but also regarding how to make citizen engagement mechanisms smoother and more effective.

In the context of this project, Edgeryders are prototyping a new form of society and a new form of citizen–institution engagement. Prototyping necessarily contains a performative element in the sense that a form of social organisation is presented and put on display as a possibility, there to be critiqued or to inspire. Ultimately that test either fails or succeeds. Here, Edgeryders are taking the initial risks in striking out with new forms of society, culture, working, learning and political participation. In order for any of these to take root and have a lasting impact, institutional support is essential. Edgeryders have made a start; institutions have the far easier job of jumping onto the successful bandwagons.

Aims beyond policy

Edgeryders has always been more than a policy research tool. It has equally been a resource for European youth. The platform has been described as a "peer-to-peer learning environment" and a source of help and inspiration, and Edgeryders have gained far more from their interactions on the edge of the policy sphere than the

---

117. Nadia, "Making sense of Edgeryders experiences: where do we go from here?: learning to live: the first Edgeryders Community Paper!!", available at http://edgeryders.ppa.coe.int/making-sense-edgeryders-experiences-where-do-we-go-here/mission_case/learning-to-live, accessed 22 July 2013.

opportunity to contribute to the next generation of youth policies. In concluding this report, it is only right to reflect on what the participants themselves have gained from their part in *Edgeryders*:

> I feel like I have learned more about genuine and fair development co-operation, trans-national networks and grassroots initiatives on Edgeryders rather than during my Master studies in International Development and feel like I have connected to [a] real-time account of the XXI Century social dynamics. ... Edgeryders has reinforced my conviction/belief that there's hope in this generation of ours and ... room to grow and improve, through the sharing of ideas and resources among peers on platforms like these. It gave me a sense of belonging to a solid and caring community. (TOOLosophy)

> I've learned that we have a lot of common aspirations that are not conditioned by national settings, by "my politician", "my university", "my potential employer", "my church", "my neighbours", even "my family". Also, aspirations are non-negotiable. Any individual, no matter what her background or opportunities, has the right and responsibility to do what she thinks is necessary to achieve them. Good news is, we stand together. (Noemi)

> I feel on the edge, I feel the victim of wrong policies ... I feel the need for more social [cohesion] ... I feel excluded from and mocked by local and national politics. [But] I feel lucky because I live the change, I feel good because I'm on the right track ... I feel good because I met a large governmental institution, Council of Europe." (SimoneMuffolini)

> This platform has been a light beacon in a dark ocean and I thank you for that. (Nirgal)

Moving forward with *Edgeryders*

One of the most important contributions to the policy-making process made by *Edgeryders* as a project and Edgeryders as individuals (as well as a community) is that of revealing a previously neglected agenda. They have asked, and in many cases answered, questions that no one else had thought to ask – or had been able to answer. Youth in Europe demonstrably have much to offer in terms of skills, knowledge, insights, and, above all, a willingness to live according to their values and principles in ways that are forging new, and arguably long overdue, social and cultural norms. *Edgeryders* presents policy makers with an invaluable opportunity to capitalise on these offerings. Yet there are still some young people, especially those on the other side of the digital divide, whose input remains more difficult to elicit. How might institutions develop innovative ways of entering into (and maintaining) dialogue with these particularly marginalised groups? Perhaps they could ask them and find out.

References

Bello, B.G. (2012), "Social inclusion of young people. Being socially included on the Edge?", Report to the Council of Europe, www.scribd.com/doc/113482202/Social-inclusion-of-young-people-Being-socially-included-on-the-Edge, accessed 20 July 2013.

Bynner, J. and Parsons, S. (2002), "Social exclusion and the transition from school to work: the case of young people Not in Education, Employment, or Training (NEET)", *Journal of Vocational Behaviour* 60(2), pp. 289-309.

Chisholm, L., Kovacheva, S. and Merico, M. (eds) (2011), "European Youth Studies: integrating research, policy and practice", EYS Consortium, Innsbruck.

Coleman, J. (1991), *Foundations of social theory*, Harvard University Press, Cambridge, MA.

Council of Europe (2008) "The future of the Council of Europe youth policy: Agenda 2020", www.coe.int/t/dg4/youth/ig_coop/8_cemry_declaration_EN.asp, accessed 20 July 2013.

Council of the European Union (2009) Resolution on a renewed framework for European cooperation in the youth field (2010-2018), Council of the European Union, Brussels, http://youth-partnership-eu.coe.int/youth-partnership/documents/EKCYP/Youth_Policy/docs/YP_strategies/Policy/doc1648_en.pdf, accessed 20 July 2013.

Council of the European Union (2005), *European Youth Pact*, Council of the European Union, Brussels.

Denstad, F.Y. (2009), *Youth Policy Manual: how to develop a national youth strategy*, Council of Europe Publishing, Strasbourg.

Devlin, M. (2010), "Young people, youth work and youth policy: European developments", *Youth Studies Ireland* 5(2), pp. 66-82.

Eriksson, M. (2012) "Political Participation Reloaded," report to the Council of Europe, published online.

European Commission (2009), *An EU Strategy for Youth – Investing and Empowering, A renewed open method of coordination to address youth challenges and opportunities*, Commission of the European Communities, Brussels, www.eur-lex.europa.eu/LexUriServ/LexUriServ.do?uri=COM:2009:0200:FIN:EN:PDF, accessed 20 July 2013.

European Commission (2001), "A New Impetus for European Youth," report by the Commission of the European Communities, Brussels, www.europa.eu/legislation_summaries/education_training_youth/youth/c11055_en.htm, accessed 20 July 2013.

EUtrio.be (2011), *The European and International Policy Agendas on Children, Youth and Children's Rights,* Belgian EU Presidency-Youth Note, www.keki.be/documents/presidencynote.pdf, accessed 20 July 2013.

Gutiérrez-Esteban, P. and Mikiewicz, P. (2012), "Learning on the Edge: Edgeryders' learning and educational experiences", report to the Council of Europe, published online.

Jeffrey, C. and McDowell, L. (2004) "Youth in a comparative perspective: global change, local lives", *Youth and Society* 36(2), pp. 131-42.

Liebau, E. and Chisholm, L. (1993), "Youth, social change and education: issues and problems", *Journal of Education Policy* 8(1), pp. 3-8.

Lieshout, H. van and Wilthagen, T. (2003), "Transitional labour markets and training: rebalancing flexibility and security for lifelong learning", López Blasco, A., McNeish, W. and Walther, A. (eds), *Young People and Contradictions of Inclusion: Towards Integrated Transition Policies in Europe*, Polity Press, Bristol.

Marcus, G. and Vickers, B. (2012), "Edgeryders: a network analysis," report to the Council of Europe, published online.

McNeish, W. and Loncle, P. (2003), "State policy and youth unemployment in the EU: rights, responsibilities and lifelong learning", López Blasco, A., McNeish, W. and Walther, A. (eds), *Young People and Contradictions of Inclusion: Towards Integrated Transition Policies in Europe*, Polity Press, Bristol.

O'Donoghue, J., Kirshner, B. and McLaughlin, M.W. (2003), "Moving youth participation forward", *New Directions for Youth Development: Theory, Practice and Research* No. 96, Jossey-Bass, San Francisco.

Potočnik, D. (2012), "Making a living reloaded", report to the Council of Europe, published online.

Putnam, R.D. (2001), *Bowling Alone: The Collapse and Revival of American Community*, Simon and Schuster, New York/London/Toronto/Sydney.

Siurala, L. (2006), "A European framework for youth policy", report from the Directorate of Youth and Sport, Council of Europe Publishing, Strasbourg.

Stauber, B., Kovacheva, S. and Lieshout, H. van (2003), "Flexibility and security: the supposed dilemma of transition policies", López Blasco, A., McNeish, W. and Walther, A. (eds), *Young People and Contradictions of Inclusion: Towards Integrated Transition Policies in Europe*, Polity Press, Bristol.

Titley, G. (2008), "The future of the Council of Europe youth policy: AGENDA 2020", unpublished Council of Europe background document, 8th Council of Europe Conference of Ministers responsible for Youth, Kyiv, Ukraine, 10-11 October 2008.

Walther, A. (2006), "Regimes of youth transitions: choice, flexibility and security in young people's experiences across different European contexts", *Young (Nordic Journal of Youth Research)* 14(2), pp. 119-39.

Walther, A. et al. (2004), "Youth policy and participation: potentials of participation and informal learning in young people's transitions to the labour market", Final report, European Commission: IRIS, Brussels.

Williamson, H. (2002), *Supporting young people in Europe: principles, policy and practice. Council of Europe international reviews of national youth policy 1997-2001 – a synthesis report*, Council of Europe Publishing, Strasbourg.

Williamson, H. (2008), *Supporting young people in Europe, Volume 2: Lessons from the "second seven" – Council of Europe international reviews of national youth policy*, Council of Europe Publishing, Strasbourg.

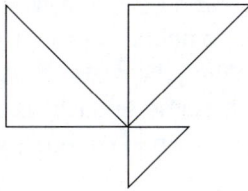

Appendix A – Engaging the citizen expert
A user's manual for the European scale

Developing an online community for the design of public policies in a complex environment: a methodological account from the Edgeryders project

Alberto Cottica[118]

Introduction

This is an overview of the methodology of the *Edgeryders* project, an open and distributed think tank of young Europeans that works through an interactive online platform. Developed by the Social Cohesion Research and Early Warning Division at the Council of Europe, *Edgeryders* was tasked with looking at the transitions of youth to independent, active life from a holistic perspective. The project has encompassed an arc of 13 months at the time of writing (September 2011 to September 2012). An unusual project that embraced the Internet as its main meeting place and locus of co-ordination for all activities, *Edgeryders* had to innovate its administrative modus operandi at every step just to stay viable. This document tries to summarise the operational knowledge gathered along the way. Its purpose is to serve as a guide for managers of future policy-oriented online communities.

---

118. Expert of online citizen engagement and open-data, http://www.cottica.net.

Rationale: the wiki government

Public policy has come under scrutiny in recent years. New global challenges loom large, from climate change to rogue finance and growing inequalities. And yet, government – humanity's primary infrastructure for collective decision making – has failed, so far, to take credible action. Even day-by-day societal and economic management seems to be slipping from the grip of our institutions. Keeping the education system in sync with the needs of the knowledge economy; estimating the costs of a large-scale event; processing a patent application within a reasonable time; all such tasks seem to have moved out of the reach of government in typical first-world countries with solid democratic institutions.[119]

Why this failure? Recent scholarly debate points to the decision-making model that stands at the core of modern public institutions. This model, codified by Max Weber, states that professionals ("the personally detached and strictly objective expert") are the only people qualified to make decisions. While citizens may express personal opinions, they lack the impartiality, expertise, resources, discipline and time for fully informed decision making. Weber's position seems hardly controversial; and yet, it has been proven time and again to be factually wrong. For example, experimental tests of the ability of experts to make predictions show them to be not significantly better than ordinary citizens, or even random predictions.[120]

In democracies, a natural way out of this dilemma is for government to turn to its citizens for help, recasting them as experts and allocating more decision-making power to them. This strategy, while helpful in some cases, was largely impractical until the Internet became pervasive. Internet tools have led to the sudden visibility of fringe interests. Likewise, it has allowed minuscule minorities to participate in debates about policy problems they know and care about (Cottica 2010; Noveck 2009).

In the past decade, loose groups of citizens collaborating on the Internet, with no command structure, no legal status and no or very few financial resources have been able to achieve impressive results. The most notable is probably the online encyclopaedia Wikipedia. At the time of writing, Wikipedia has about 23 million articles in

---

119. The budget for the London 2012 Olympics closed at £9.3 billion, almost four times the amount estimated in 2005, when the city made its successful hosting bid (BBC 2012). Noveck (2009) reports that a patent application in the United States takes an average of over three years to be processed.
120. See Watts (2011). In most experiments the predictions of experts are significantly worse than that of educated non-experts, and experts make worse predictions in their areas of expertise. In almost all cases, a simple statistical model makes better predictions than the experts.

280 languages online, all produced and maintained by 1.5 million active editors.[121] Allocating so many people to so many different tasks is a titanic task of co-ordination; Wikipedia's software and the social conventions that go with it resolve this by simply allowing each person to decide which article they want to contribute to, and when. This guarantees that each Wikipedian positions herself exactly where she can have the most impact with the least effort: editing articles on topics she is knowledgeable or passionate about, for instance. The information on who is best paired with what article is not stored anywhere in the system. It is, rather, an emergent property of Wikipedia itself.

This approach, influenced by complexity science and Internet culture, is being applied to many areas of public policy, including street maintenance, intelligence, firm creation in lagging areas, processing patent applications, online citizen consultation and scrutiny by crowdsourced inspection of government data (Cottica 2010). The degree of success has been varied, but most observers agree the approach is promising enough to persist with.

Context: youth in transition

In the summer of 2011, the Council of Europe and the European Commission agreed to co-fund a project called "Youth in Transition". The idea was to explore the condition of young Europeans, portrayed by the media as a "lost generation". Many statistical indicators (youth unemployment rate, NEET rate, turnout at elections, and so on) seemed to support such a view. What does qualitative research have to say?

This question and its deployment in the form of a project were the brainchild of the Social Cohesion Research and Early Warning Division. The Division's management suspected that the "lost generation" story was skewed by measuring young Europeans by the yardstick of the older generation. This, in turn, could lead to stigmatising the young, writing them down as a problem to solve.

In this context, the wiki government approach held one clear advantage: it would inevitably embed the voice of the young themselves in the final output. By virtue of its transparency and openness, it greatly reduced the risk of adopting a stigmatising point of view towards the new generations: the latter would notice and voice their disagreement.

There was also a cultural disadvantage. The Council of Europe was established in 1949 by a diplomatic treaty, in a cultural and ideological climate very different from today, and is still largely organised as a Weberian bureaucracy. Furthermore, it sees its role

---

121. Source: http://stats.wikimedia.org/EN/TablesWikipediaZZ.htm, accessed 20 July 2013. The number of editors does not include people who contribute anonymously and without creating an account, known as "good Samaritans" in Wikipedia parlance.

as that of a top-level international regulator, starting from prime principles of human rights, democracy and rule of law and drafting from these, policy recommendations for its member states. Recent evolutions in legal doctrine around the issues of transparency and openness of government have prompted the Council of Europe to recommend to member states and its own corporate structure that they "ensure a bolder and more substantial input from civil society at large on topical societal issues. Thematic interaction should be organised around platforms related to priority themes" (Council of Europe 2010).

Despite this, as of 2011 no attempt had been made by the Council of Europe to elicit citizen input through online social media. The Organisation does maintain a blog (with closed comments) and a Facebook and Twitter account, but they are designed strictly to repackage content produced in-house and broadcast it to the web. In fact, the nuts and bolts of its internal policy for corporate web presence make it quite difficult for the Council of Europe to fully engage with citizens on the Internet. For example:

- all content on the Council of Europe websites is copyrighted. The use of Creative Commons or other open licenses is implicitly forbidden. Apparently, no one had ever wondered if claiming legal rights on content contributed by citizens is appropriate practice for a public institution;

- at the time of the rolling out of "Youth in Transition", no corporate server existed with an open source stack of software that supported the most common free/open social software (Wordpress, Drupal, Wikimedia, and so on);

- the organisation lacks internal guidelines for the use of social media by staff members;

- design guidelines for corporate website design do not allow the hybridisation of the corporate identity. In the case of *Edgeryders* this problem was circumvented by affirming the project's identity as a so-called joint programme between the Council of Europe and the European Commission, which meant it was not subject to those rules.[122]

If these operational difficulties can be overcome, however, the Council of Europe's significant advantages in engaging with the citizenry at large could come into play:

- it sees itself as the champion of human rights and democracy, foundational values of the European civilisation and dear to the heart of a great many Europeans;

122. In May 2012, as *Edgeryders* came to a close, the IT directorate issued a new regulation that mandates not only a particular type of design, but the underlying technology as well – for all corporate websites including joint programmes. The stated aim of this move is to obtain "long-term savings". This, however, might have the immediate effect of stifling internal innovation, making projects like *Edgeryders* impossible.

- its clear distance from vested interests appeals to those citizens who feel big business is overrepresented in the governance of the European project;

- with 47 member states and 800 million citizens, it connects a truly pan-European community, beyond the borders of the EU;

- it has the administrative infrastructure critical to managing long-distance interactions with citizens. Funding trips of third party experts to Strasbourg to attend meetings and seminars, as well as issuing small contracts, is routine fare for the Council of Europe.

Despite a not completely favourable corporate culture, the *Edgeryders* project was received reasonably well by the Organisation. Fruitful collaborations were achieved with some units. *Edgeryders* even received some attention from senior management looking into possible applications of the same methodology to other areas of intervention of the Council of Europe.

The architecture of trust

The *Edgeryders* social contract: designing weak incentives

In this context, the Council of Europe decided in August 2011 to frame the Youth in Transition project as a wiki government one: a think tank of self-selected citizen experts would be tasked with exploring the problem and developing recommendations. The project was renamed *Edgeryders*.

The project required the Council of Europe to enlist the collaboration of other entities, and reward them for their effort. One such entity is the European Commission, Directorate of General Employment and Social Cohesion, which provided the bulk of the funding for the project (it had a budget of €401 000, of which €300 000 was provided by the Commission and the remaining €101 000 came from the Council of Europe's own budget). The relationship between the two institutions is regulated by a written contract, in which the signatories agree on the scope of the work (investigating the transition of young people to adult life in a time of crisis), the funding provided and the deliverables. The contract lists two of the latter: a final document containing recommendations for policy to facilitate and smoothen the transition in question; and a conference.

The other entities involved are, of course, citizens. The social contract between exercises like *Edgeryders* and participants stems from the following assumptions:

- the citizenry as a whole contains more information and expertise than any small group of experts ("nobody is smarter than everybody" – Shirky 2008);

- it is impossible to know a priori what relevant information might be out there, or which citizens have it;

- a large number of ordinary citizens will suffer from less of a cognitive bias than a small number of professional experts (Watts 2011);

- citizens are constantly prompted for "collaboration" exercises by government authorities that share very little power, and end up being little more than window dressing. Over time, this has damaged the credibility of even well-meaning institutional agents as they try to engage the citizenry.

The first assumption provides the rationale for the participation of citizens as experts in policy design; the second assumption dictates that such participation be open, enabling any individual who feels she has something to contribute to select herself to join in; the third assumption dictates that its scale be large; the final assumption that *Edgeryders* provides a more credible alternative than past or existing exercises. Taken together, the first three assumptions imply self-regulation, with participants deciding whether and how to contribute, with no top-down control other than freezing the accounts of individuals reported as abusive. In a self-regulated social environment, monetary incentives are difficult to deploy, because the sums involved could become large (for instance, Wikipedia has 27 million registered users) and because there is no easy, uncontroversial way to measure the quality of the contributions to ensure fairness and disincentivise strategic behaviour. Furthermore, in most countries public sector agencies must follow lengthy (and costly) procedures to spend their money on accountability grounds.

With monetary incentives ruled out, the *Edgeryders* team attempted to make a case for citizens to participate in the exercise by promoting an ethics of civic engagement. Three promises were made:

- participants experiencing trouble in making their own transition from youth to adulthood could get help in the form of advice from other participants;

- participants who enjoy mentoring others would have the chance to give advice;

- everyone's voice would be heard with respect and contribute to a document of policy recommendations that would be legitimised by the role and prestige of the Council of Europe.

These promises were made very publicly and in writing, in the "About" page of the *Edgeryders* blog, launched in September 2011.[123] The first two translate into the Council of Europe committing to fostering a friendly, empathetic online environment where

---

123. http://edgeryders.eu/page/about-edgeryders, accessed 22 July 2013.

individual journeys would be made sense of in light of macro-scale social and economic phenomena. For example, many participants experience precarious employment; by comparing notes across different cases and different countries, they were able to explain some of the precarity as the product of impersonal forces rather than of their own failings. The third is a promise of political empowerment: the Council of Europe was committing to augmenting the participant's influence over the political discourse by embedding their views into a formalised policy-making process. The primal trust-building exercise was the Council of Europe, a large intergovernmental institution, showing signs of accepting the work style of youth in the connected age in a visible, credible way. Through visual language, the adoption of a personal communication style and of many-to-many conversations, and the involvement of individuals credible in their own communities (see below), the Organisation was able to position itself for an alternative approach.

Later in the process, the *Edgeryders* team proposed that the project conference involve some members of the community (initially 50), invited as "citizen experts": their travel and subsistence would be funded by the project. The team agreed that being invited as an expert by an international institution would constitute a concrete sign of recognition of the high value of participation, and would have a large positive impact on motivation to participate. Furthermore, the effect would spread even to people who would not, ultimately, receive an invitation, as it would demonstrate openness. After the proposal was accepted, the team attempted a more specific social contract with participants. In order to qualify for paid travel, participants would need to commit to writing at least three mission reports. This was framed as a necessary but not sufficient condition of eligibility. The idea worked well, and a decision was reached to triple the number of funded travels to 150, so in practice everybody who wanted an invitation got one. Also, the condition was never strictly enforced, nor was it meant to be (the team sent out invitation emails mentioning "mutual commitment"). Again, this commitment was made publicly and in writing at the beginning of April 2012. The conference took place on 14 and 15 June 2012 in Strasbourg.

Design principles

Having decided to approach the Youth in Transition project with an open government stance, the team proceeded to design its specific methodology, starting with key principles to guide operational choices. These were:

-   self-selection: *Edgeryders* is open to everyone, and refused to set participation limits or quotas (by age, nationality, educational achievement or other parameters). The underlying assumption is that whoever wants to engage with the Council of Europe on the issue of youth transitions is the right person to do so, because everyone has some first-hand knowledge to contribute. Most participants are themselves young; others might have young children, or siblings, or friends. This allows for intrinsic motivation to be the primary driver of participation, and builds a reactive, enthusiastic community;

— free software: *Edgeryders* needs social software to connect young Europeans scattered across the globe. For reasons of accountability, the team did not feel comfortable entrusting the data encoding citizen–institution collaboration to a for-profit corporate like Facebook or Ning. The obvious choice was to reuse and customise free and open source software: in this case, a Drupal-based general purpose social networking platform called Social Commons;[124]

— Euro English (and respect): like all international organisations, the Council of Europe takes multilingualism very seriously and promotes language diversity. However, language diversity risks fragmenting and "freezing" the online conversation that is the social engine of the whole exercise. Three solutions were implemented. The first was to build one-click Google Translate integration into the platform. The second was to establish the social norm that writing in any language is fine; however, people who know a little English are encouraged to write in English, to facilitate reading and commenting from other participants thus make the greatest impact. The third is to establish a social norm of respect with regards to language skills;

— evolutionary design: the *Edgeryders* platform co-evolved with its community, taking into account patterns of usage and user feedback, and adapting to deliver a better experience. After the alpha version (October 2011) and a major redevelopment between November 2011 and January 2012, small changes and improvements were rolled out almost continuously throughout the project: for example, support for creating teams was added in the run-up to the final conference.

The team

The *Edgeryders* team consisted of a core team of two people allocated full time to the project, a director and a creative director; a community manager (20% of the time); an engagement team (three people, each at 20%). Website development and customisation was contracted out. The Council of Europe provided administrative assistance and office facilities for the core team and a research team, recruited on a per-paper basis.

Recruiting the community by self-selection and keeping it engaged was the responsibility of the engagement team. It consisted of three people, chosen for their online and

---

124. http://acquia.com/products-services/acquia-commons-social-business-software, accessed 22 June 2013.

offline communication skills and their personal networks in spaces of interest to the project: social innovation/social enterprise, open government, resilience and lifestyle hacking. Engagement managers were asked to (a) involve their respective communities and (b) act as their reference point on the *Edgeryders* platform itself, engaging them in conversation. Most of the recruitment happened online, through social networks – predominantly Twitter and Facebook. At the time of writing, there had already been 71 000 visits to the *Edgeryders* website, of which 38 000 came through links found elsewhere on the web. Of these, 13 000 came from Twitter and 12 000 from Facebook. The core team was based in Strasbourg; of the engagement managers, two were in the UK (one was later replaced by a person based in Austria), and one in Canada. The community manager was based in Romania. The team was co-ordinated through a mailing list and occasional online meetings on Skype or Google Hangout. Two physical meetings, in the space of 18 months, were also convened in Strasbourg.

The outreach followed a simple, cost-effective design of "a tweet a day". Every day, the team would choose an interesting piece of content on the *Edgeryders* platform (typically a mission report); this would be communicated to the whole team via the internal mailing list, and everyone would get word out through social networks, Twitter especially. Engagement managers were key in this, due to their relatively large number of followers (2 000 to 3 000 each) and credibility in their respective communities. It is estimated that more than 1 400 different Twitter users mentioned *Edgeryders* on Twitter over 15 000 times from September 2011 to end of June 2012.

Team members (most of whom enjoy a relatively high profile in their own communities) lent their personal credibility to the Council of Europe's outreach effort. In order to get them to stand for the project and not just work for it, they have been managed with a light touch, encouraged to take initiatives and allowed to make mistakes. For example, one of the engagement managers spent a considerable amount of time trying to engage large youth organisations such as the scout movements and AIESEC. The management of these organisations did in general show interest and in some cases reached out to their memberships via newsletters and other means, but the contact resulted in practically no active users from those organisations.

An offline innovation: the Living on the Edge conference

The Council of Europe had committed to delivering a conference as part of the *Edgeryders* project. This had initially been envisioned as a more or less traditional dissemination event attended by professional experts and members of the policy community; however, along the way it was recast as a workspace for the *Edgeryders* community, and as a facilitated meeting ground for institutions and Europe's young citizens, across the (increasingly called into question) border between policy makers and policy beneficiaries. The conference was titled Living on the Edge. It is worth noting that:

— the conference was allocated an important share of the total budget (€95 000, or 25%);

— the list of invitees was built through an open call on the web. Citizens who felt they had something to contribute were invited as experts. The Council of Europe offered a limited amount of funded travel to those who committed to contributing, not only by attending the conference, but also by engaging on the *Edgeryders* platform in the form of mission reports;

— the agenda was carefully designed so that the conference would maintain an institutional character while opening itself up to voices of citizens, up to and including the openly dissenting ones. Breakout sessions on research issues were built into the programme; session facilitators were recruited from the community;

— it included some techno-social practices borrowed from hackers' events: a lot of attention was paid to ensuring a smooth Internet connection; systematic social media coverage was deployed by volunteers from the community; and a Twitter wall was adopted as a backchannel of participation. People could interact with the designated speakers through Twitter; their tweets were aggregated through a free online service and displayed on a giant screen behind the speakers;

— critically, the community was encouraged to set up its own event back-to-back with the official conference. Titled EdgeCamp, it took the BarCamp format, and was organised in collaboration with Alsace Digitale, an association of digital entrepreneurs based in Strasbourg.

Living on the Edge and EdgeCamp were impressive successes. The former provided a respectful, yet frank meeting space for representatives of institutions and young citizens, many of them precarious, or poor, or living outside the mainstream (two of the attendees declared themselves stateless and refused to use state-issued ID; one of them is also moneyless, and reportedly has not touched money for three years, living in a sort of one-man gift economy). By acknowledging attendees as citizen experts, the Council of Europe showed in a very concrete way attention and willingness to engage. As for EdgeCamp, some of its sessions resulted in very concrete policy proposals from the *Edgeryders* community.[125] From a communication point of view, the double event was also a success. It became a Twitter trending topic in London, and garnered a lot

---

125. The open letter to funders of innovation (demsoc, http://edgeryders.wikispiral.org/help-build-june-conference/mission_case/funding-20-edgecamp-session-dear-funders-letter) and the (un)Monastery project (http://edgeryders.ppa.coe.int/mine-becomes-ours/mission_case/few-us-living-together-somewhere-and-changing-things-unmonastery) were both results of EdgeCamp sessions.

of attention from young changemakers. Figure 3 shows the accelerating growth in mission reports and comments after the conference was announced in early April 2012. A strong acceleration is clearly visible in the run-up to and immediate aftermath of the Living on the Edge conference; in August, with the project focusing on research papers, a slump is recorded.

The greatest value of Living on the Edge has probably been to give credibility to the inclusive stance of the whole *Edgeryders* project. The conference was announced in early April, and gave fresh impulse to new sign-ups and content upload. We recommend developing this prototype further, as there is a clear need for spaces of interaction between institutions and unmediated citizens that are inclusive and respectful, and yet do not deny conflicts or unpleasant truths.

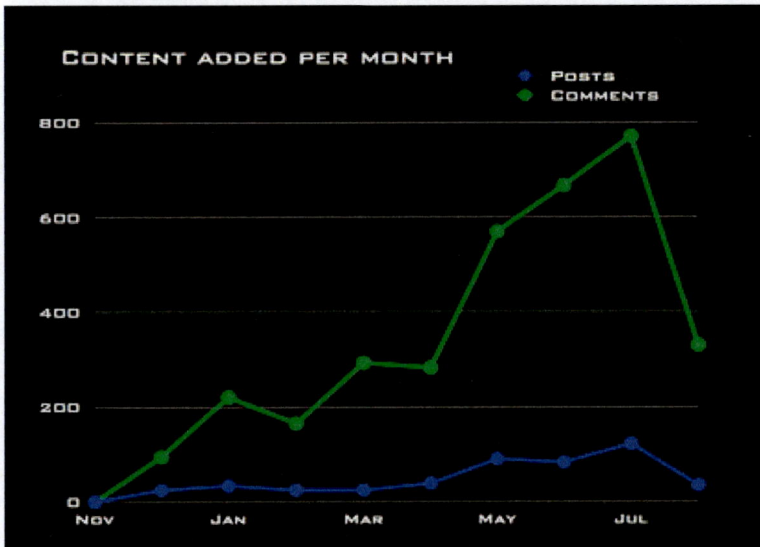

Figure 3: *Edgeryders* submitted content over time

Drawing conclusions: open science

The *Edgeryders* project adopts an open science stance. The idea is to release valuable data from the project into the public domain, where scholars can reuse them, and perhaps add to the analysis done by the project's own research team. This stance has its roots in the open data movement, and is fully consistent with European regulations on the reusability of public sector information; information collected in the course of the *Edgeryders* project, after all, was paid for by taxpayer money, and taxpayers have a right to reuse it if they choose to do so. In the context of participatory projects like *Edgeryders*, openness takes on additional value as it helps to build trust and gives the community a feeling of greater control over how they are portrayed in the reports.

Netnography

At the time of writing, the *Edgeryders* database contains more than 500 mission reports and nearly 4 000 comments. As a way to sift through the content, two young sociologists were tasked with coming up with an online ethnography of the *Edgeryders* community. Online ethnography, or "netnography", seems to be a good fit for exercises in participatory democracy for two reasons. First, ethnographic studies are constructed to include the point of view of the community being studied; that is what defines them. Second, online interaction comes with first-person statements by the community being studied, in writing; this is arguably the most expensive part of ethnographic research.

The methodology of this study is explained in detail by the researchers themselves. What matters here is the openness: the study started by reading through the content and assigning tags called "codes" to particularly relevant pieces of content. This is done using a software called WEFT-QDA, and the files were published on the *Edgeryders* website for the convenience of other scholars.

Monitoring social dynamics

A network analysis of the *Edgeryders* community has been published, wherein the *Edgeryders* conversation was modelled as a network of comments (A connects to B if A comments on B's content). The platform contains a functionality that exports the results of any database query as a file in a format called JSON, amenable to parsing and analysis. Open source developers have written software that parse the JSON files and encode them in file formats that standard network analysis software can read. Both the network extraction code and an anonymised dataset are available online for the use of any interested researcher.[126]

Close monitoring of the relationships on the *Edgeryders* platform has been a valuable management tool for the following reasons:

–   to identify more easily the most central members of the community;

–   to assess the work done by the project team in connecting community members and enhancing their experience (Figure 4);

---

126. https://github.com/dragontrainer/edgeryders-mapper, accessed 20 July 2013.

- to make an educated guess about the sustainability of the conversation (would it keep going if we suddenly removed the contribution of the team?) and its scalability (does it stay manageable as the number of participants and the quantity of shared material increase?) (Cottica 2012a, 2012b);

- the impact of management decisions can also be assessed quantitatively, improving accountability. For example, it seems likely that the sequential structure by campaign (a broad issue was launched for discussion every four weeks) has channelled the conversation into sub-communities that have self-organised at different points in time. The community's growth seems to have resulted in the growth of the number of sub-communities, rather than in the increased (and overwhelming) interaction of everyone with everyone else.

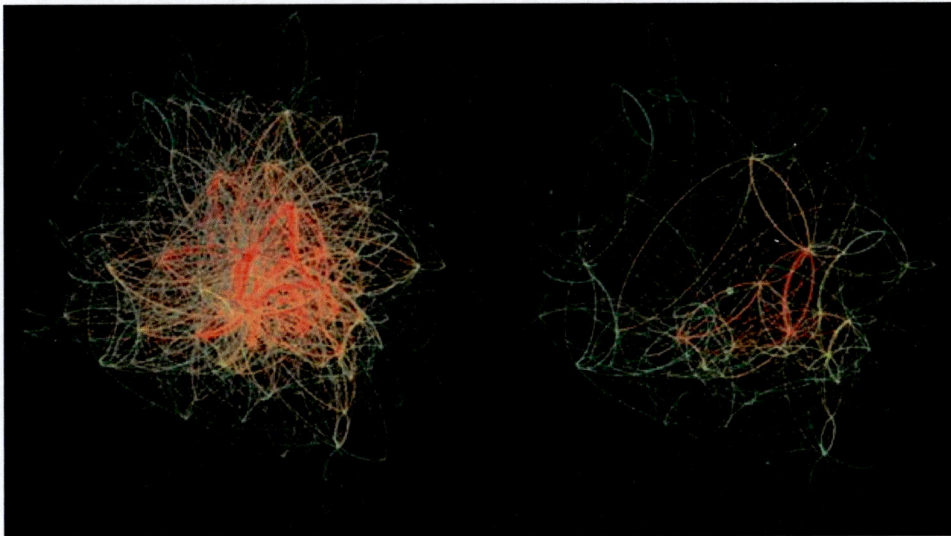

Figure 4: Visualisation of the *Edgeryders* network with and without the project team

Note: The full *Edgeryders* network is depicted on the left, and the "induced conversation" involving only community members but not the project team on the right. Redder colours represent comments by more central members of the *Edgeryders* community.

A prototype for engaging citizens online?

Edgeryders could be a prototype for online citizen engagement at the European level, well beyond the youth policy context that generated it. Traditionally, citizen engagement at the European level is done through representative agents for the stakeholders (for example, trade associations representing businesses, or trade unions representing workers), holding large offline meetings, where – inevitably, given the scale – few people talk and many are talked to. This setup has many flaws. The most obvious are:

- representation works relatively well in simple, massified societies, but not in 21st-century Europe, where the legitimacy of all representation is declining fast;

- even when representation works well, using representative agents in modern sociology is deprecated, because representative agents assume away all of the complex phenomena arising from the interaction between many agents (Watts 2011). For example, "the banking sector" might benefit from a stable environment, but all the agency is the hands of individual banks, which stand to gain a lot from market instability and are likely to try to push the system towards it;

- meetings do not scale: involving more people tends to dampen the interaction between any two participants;

- meetings are expensive and hard to organise, so they tend to be few and far between, as well as highly ritualised.

Edgeryders can claim, at least in theory, superiority in each of these areas:

- There is no representation. Participants represent themselves, and their experience is validated by their peers.

- Interaction happens mostly online – and, as we have seen, online interaction scales relatively well. To date, about 250 members of the *Edgeryders* community have actively contributed content (counting only mission reports and comments on the *Edgeryders* platform). So, all other things being equal, many more people can be active in online participatory environments. This is valuable, because human cognition is affected by many biases (framing, anchoring, confirmation bias, motivated reasoning, loss aversion, halo effect and many others), and at least some of them cancel each other out when a large number of respondents are pulled together.

- Another positive side effect of online interaction is the diversity of participation. Online, it is more difficult to display the markers of social status; as a result, people feel it is acceptable to interact across all kinds of social divides.[127] All other things being equal, diversity not only is desirable per se, it helps to reduce further the cognitive biases associated with all participants looking, so to speak, in the same direction.

---

127. The very first public policy designed by citizens online, in 1989, was the (unintended) result of a collaboration between homeless and homed citizens who would have never interacted offline (Van Tassel 1994).

-   Interaction online is vastly more traceable and measurable than its offline counterpart. Everything that happens on the *Edgeryders* interactive platform is encoded in its database: this means having a perfect and instantly verifiable collective memory of who has been saying what. This improves trust among participants, improves accountability for institutions, and is amenable to precisely set and easily verifiable quantitative measurements of the project's performance (for example, "we want each mission report to receive at least two comments", or "the average number of interactions of all users on the platform must be at least 10").

-   Once put on the web, all knowledge produced becomes much easier to reuse. Thanks to an open science/open data stance, *Edgeryders* is potentially able to help scholars, researchers and citizens in the future.

-   Finally, participation on the web is asynchronous, always-on and cheap to maintain. There is no need to wait for the next conference to make a point or ask a question, nor is there need to sit through an uninteresting presentation to get to an interesting one.

Given the scale and physical distances involved, the team proposes online communities as a general purpose tool for citizen engagement at the European level. *The Edgeryders* experience suggests that physical conferences like Living on the Edge fit very well in an online engagement model, boosting participation that the online platform will channel and archive.

Suggested improvements

Understanding each other: the meeting of two worlds

The *Edgeryders* project showed how citizens and officials feel the need for a frank, constructive dialogue with each other. However, it was not completely successful in designing a platform that supported this dialogue in a satisfying way for everyone.

On the online platform, dialogue has been, indeed, frank and constructive. It has resulted in high-quality research and several concrete and innovative proposals. However, such dialogue happened by proxy; outside the *Edgeryders* team, no one in the Council of Europe or the European Commission has engaged with the community on their own terms, that is, by creating an account and writing.

Living on the Edge performed better in this respect; there was interaction across the institutional divide, and the community had been socialised to what constructive conversation is in the context of the project. However, some of its more radical (and creative) members felt that the agenda was still disproportionately allocated to "political speech" from senior officials and elected representatives, and that the discussion, both in style and in content, revealed there was still unwillingness to face hard truths and propose bold, radical measures.

We suggest allocating more resources to internal championing of the methodology – which already has more acceptability than it did in 2011. A better knowledge of the project on the part of more people in the Organisation will lead to more online participation and more creativity in designing online interaction. More active involvement from more colleagues would certainly reinforce the project's narrative of constructive collaboration.

Proximity to public decision making

Edgeryders is a consultative exercise: it has no mandate whatsoever to make decisions. Citizen collaboration is invoked to produce a policy document, but no one can promise that the recommendations in that document will become policy. The pay-off of democratic participation could be increased by attaching it to a concrete decision: this would empower citizens, making them feel that they have influenced a real-life decision maker making a real-life decision. While there is added value in comparing notes at the European scale (and therefore it makes sense that the community is European) the decision itself need not be. A local decision would work too, especially if seen as an experience that could then be scaled up through European-level networks of local governments.

Time profile

The time profile of the *Edgeryders* project (four months for design, internal selling and testing; eight months for citizen engagement; six months for research and writing the recommendations) is not necessarily best suited to building a large-scale community and reaping its benefits. For example, the project went into shutdown mode just at the time of peak community activity; it would have been more efficient to keep the engagement going to reap more data. The team recommends a two- or three-year time frame for *Edgeryders*-style projects (with decreasing funding) to climb the learning curve.

Privacy

Online privacy is a thorny issue. Several respected members of the *Edgeryders* community refuse to use Facebook, or use it sparingly, and the decision to run *Edgeryders* from an entirely government-funded and self-hosted platform was well received. As is often the case on the Internet, openness and privacy are somewhat at odds with each other, and this restlessness has occasionally surfaced on *Edgeryders*.[128] The team's response was to encourage the community to design rules that they felt were acceptable: trust creation trumps data granularity in this case. So, if even a few people in the community are not comfortable with a particular form of open science, they can engage in discussions until a solution is found that everybody can live with. This stance seems to have worked well, and is recommended for future engagement projects.

Continuity: designing for a spin-off?

There are signs that *Edgeryders* might develop into a sustainable model of citizen engagement at the crossroads between consultancy and citizen consultation. It has the attitude for solution design of the former, and the openness of the latter, and it could be deployed to help policy decisions in various contexts. In fact, since the Living on the Edge conference the community has been discussing the possibility of spinning itself off from the mother project to form a non-profit think tank.[129] If this were to really happen, it would be prestigious for the Council of Europe: it would prove that *Edgeryders* as a policy is really demand driven – so much so that citizens adopt it as their own initiative. The *Edgeryders* community should be encouraged in this effort.

References

BBC (2012), "London Olympics 'to come in £476m under budget'", www.bbc.co.uk/news/uk-politics-18421211, accessed 22 July 2013.

Cottica, A. (2010), *Wikicrazia. L'azione di governo al tempo della rete: capirla, progettarla, viverla da protagonist*, Navarra Editore, Palermo.

Cottica, A. (2012a), "How online conversations scale, and why this matters for public policies", www.cottica.net/2012/08/01/how-online-conversations-scale-and-why-this-matters-for-public-policies, accessed 22 July 2013.

Cottica, A. (2012b), "Is your online community sustainable? A network science approach", www.cottica.net/2012/08/20/is-your-online-community-sustainable-a-network-science-approach, accessed 22 July 2013.

---

128. See in particular this discussion: http://edgeryders.ppa.coe.int/spotlight-internet-common-resource/mission_case/what-can-happen-your-edgeryders-data-and-you, accessed 22 July 2013.
129. See this discussion: http://edgeryders.ppa.coe.int/where-edgeryders-dare/mission_case/can-we-and-should-we-pull-official-edgeryders-organisation, accessed 22 July 2013.

Council of Europe (2010), "New Council of Europe engagement with civil society", Information DocumentsSG/Inf(2010)21, – www.wcd.coe.int/ViewDoc.jsp?id=1702437&Site=CM, accessed 22 July 2013.

Noveck, B. (2009), *The Wiki Government*, Brookings Institutions Press, Washington, DC.

Shirky, C. (2008), *Here Comes Everybody: The Power of Organizing Without Organizations*, Penguin Press: London.

Van Tassel, J. (1994), "Yakety-yak, do talk back!", *Wired,* www.wired.com/wired/archive/2.01/pen_pr.html, accessed 22 July 2013.

Watts, D. (2011), *Everything is obvious (once you know the answer)*, Crown Business, New York.

Weber, M. (1991), *Essays in sociology* (eds Gerth, H.H. and Mills, C.W.), Routledge, Oxford.

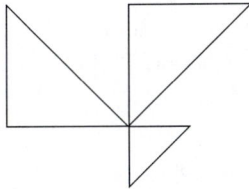

Appendix B – An open letter to funders and supporters of innovation

This letter was collaboratively drafted by participants in the EdgeCamp Unconference and the Council of Europe's Edgeryders conference in June, and in online discussions thereafter. It represents the views of all those who took part in its drafting.

Dear Funders (and other supporters of innovation)

It's just not working out.

The way that you provide support for innovation isn't working for you, or for us. We don't like the bureaucratic processes, high organisational requirements and over-specified funding calls – and we are sure that you don't like administering them either. The financial and social crisis is making reform and agile innovation even more important, but processes are still slow.

We'd like to find a better way to get support and resources to innovators who can make change happen, a way that's less bureaucratic but weeds out bad ideas by letting them fail quickly and cheaply.

We know it's a bit self-interested, because most of the people who signed this letter are innovators themselves – we're writing it at the EdgeCamp/Edgeryders Unconference in Strasbourg. But we think it's in your interests too, because you have complex social goals you want to meet, but you aren't working in ways that create complex solutions.

So, we want to have a proper conversation with you about resourcing innovation differently, but here are some ideas to start with:

Fund networked people, not organisations

None of the social problems that we face can be solved by single solutions, so we should start to focus on building up networks of ideas and initiatives (old and new). The sorts of successful innovation network we should emulate include: Las Indias,[130] Open Source Ecology,[131] and the Arduino Community.[132]

Look for ideas that have already got community support

We think crowdfunding has potential to be expanded. Crowdfunding demonstrates that an idea has community support before it even starts. We could work on a matched crowdfunding platform for innovation. Like the Unlimited programme in the UK, Goteo[133] in Spain or CrowdCulture[134] in Sweden, innovators could propose an idea and get pledges of cash or in-kind support from the community that it's intended to benefit, and then those contributions could be matched or increased by your resources.

Give people time to think, not money to spend

Lots of innovators have to take temporary work to fund their lives while they develop their ideas, but finding temporary work is time-consuming. Rather than providing cash for spending, funders could support people's living expenses for a certain period of time – like a bursary or a sabbatical from a university. This is already happening with one project run by Alsace Digitale[135] and is also the logic behind the successful Ashoka.org programmes on "social entrepreneurship".

Tell us what you need, and support us as you see solutions evolve

Challenge-driven funding models encourage the creation of solutions that actually work. Small grants could be given to a number of applicants to enable them to develop advanced prototypes, and following waves of funding would only be available for the most promising ones. This kind of "create-then-fund" mechanism makes money

130. http://english.lasindias.com, accessed 23 July 2013.
131. http://opensourceecology.org, accessed 23 July 2013.
132. http://arduino.cc, accessed 23 July 2013.
133. http://goteo.org, accessed 23 July 2013.
134. www.guerrilla-innovation.com/archives/2011/07/000798.php, accessed 23 July 2013.
135. www.alsacedigitale.org, accessed 23 July 2013.

follow results, not the opposite, crowding away the "experts in proposal writing" and attracting the innovative "doers".

Think whole-system

Find organisations that can lead local action that has positive impacts across multiple priorities, and try to avoid focusing on specific outputs. Focusing on outputs presumes that your funding priority can be severed from the rest of the community's actions, and that you truly know the situation on the ground. It can't and you don't – but local community organisations often do. Find ways to receive as well as produce information, and don't assume best practice in one community is applicable to another – the fine details matter.

Support places where innovation and connection can happen

We'd like to see funding for a network of simple, cheap spaces where innovation can happen, and then we'll put regular meet-ups and events in them. We don't mean shiny well-staffed co-working spaces, just a simple space with good Wi-Fi that can be used for regular events. Kultwerk West in Hamburg is a good example of the space we mean, and Third Thursday in Brighton the sort of event. If there were a Kultwerk in every big city, we'd know where to make connections into local innovators.

Interoperability and collaboration as the default

We want to create tools that work with each other, and where collaboration is the default setting. We take inspiration from well-known initiatives such as the Open Knowledge Foundation[136] and Free Software Foundation,[137] but also less famous collectives like Riseup[138] – providing autonomous secure services for over 4m people and working closely with UNICEF, and Unhosted[139] – developing open technologies addressing issues of web monopolies and with support of NLnet and TERENA started providing RemoteStorage-based services to universities in Europe.

Developments in the field of distributed social networking and linked data have started maturing, and offer solutions for overcoming not only technical obstacles but also many linguistic and cultural barriers. Participants in institutions like DERI[140] or AKSW[141] (both

136. http://okfn.org, accessed 23 July 2013.
137. http://fsf.org, accessed 23 July 2013.
138. http://riseup.net/en, accessed 23 July 2013.
139. http://unhosted.org, accessed 23 July 2013.
140. http://deri.ie, accessed 23 July 2013.
141. http://wiki.aksw.org/About, accessed 23 July 2013.

funded by the EU's FP7[142]) with their infrastructure could dedicate even more focus to support development of distributed collaboration and sharing tools. With broad and diverse support for such collaborations we could expect development of more projects supporting civic involvement like in the case of Code for America – sometimes referred to as "a peace corps for geeks".

Conclusion

We don't think these ideas are the answer, but we think they are different aspects of the answer: ways of looking at problems that emphasise openness, collaboration, whole-system thinking and trusting, productive collaboration.

We think you will want to have a conversation about resourcing innovation differently as well. We're ready, online and in person, when you are.

We hope to hear from you soon.

Signed

The Edgeryders and EdgeCampers
Anthony Zacharzewski – The Democratic Society (UK)
Pedro Prieto-Martín – Asociación Ciudades Kyosei (ES)
Nadia El-Imam – Edgeryders (BE), @Ladyniasan
Arthur Doohan (IE)
Lyne Robichaud (Quebec, Canada)
Ola Möller – Idea Society (SE)
elf Pavlik – hackers4peace (stateless nomad)
Maxime Lathuilière – OuiShare/Ars Industrialis (FR)
Nicolas Hel (FR)
and other contributors who did not want to be named.

This letter was based on a mission report posted as "Funding 2.0 Edgecamp session: 'Dear Funders' letter", available at http://edgeryders.wikispiral.org/help-build-june-conference/mission_case/funding-20-edgecamp-session-dear-funders-letter.

---

142. http://cordis.europa.eu/fp7/home_en.html, accessed 23 July 2013.

Sales agents for publications of the Council of Europe
Agents de vente des publications du Conseil de l'Europe

BELGIUM/BELGIQUE
La Librairie Européenne -
The European Bookshop
Rue de l'Orme, 1
BE-1040 BRUXELLES
Tel.: +32 (0)2 231 04 35
Fax: +32 (0)2 735 08 60
E-mail: info@libeurop.eu
http://www.libeurop.be

Jean De Lannoy/DL Services
Avenue du Roi 202 Koningslaan
BE-1190 BRUXELLES
Tel.: +32 (0)2 538 43 08
Fax: +32 (0)2 538 08 41
E-mail: jean.de.lannoy@dl-servi.com
http://www.jean-de-lannoy.be

**BOSNIA AND HERZEGOVINA/
BOSNIE-HERZÉGOVINE**
Robert's Plus d.o.o.
Marka Marulića 2/V
BA-71000 SARAJEVO
Tel.: + 387 33 640 818
Fax: + 387 33 640 818
E-mail: robertsplus@bih.net.ba

CANADA
Renouf Publishing Co. Ltd.
22-1010 Polytek Street
CDN-OTTAWA, ONT K1J 9J1
Tel.: +1 613 745 2665
Fax: +1 613 745 7660
Toll-Free Tel.: (866) 767-6766
E-mail: order.dept@renoufbooks.com
http://www.renoufbooks.com

CROATIA/CROATIE
Robert's Plus d.o.o.
Marasovićeva 67
HR-21000 SPLIT
Tel.: + 385 21 315 800, 801, 802, 803
Fax: + 385 21 315 804
E-mail: robertsplus@robertsplus.hr

**CZECH REPUBLIC/
RÉPUBLIQUE TCHÈQUE**
Suweco CZ, s.r.o.
Klecakova 347
CZ-180 21 PRAHA 9
Tel.: +420 2 424 59 204
Fax: +420 2 848 21 646
E-mail: import@suweco.cz
http://www.suweco.cz

DENMARK/DANEMARK
GAD
Vimmelskaftet 32
DK-1161 KØBENHAVN K
Tel.: +45 77 66 60 00
Fax: +45 77 66 60 01
E-mail: reception@gad.dk
http://www.gad.dk

FINLAND/FINLANDE
Akateeminen Kirjakauppa
PO Box 128
Keskuskatu 1
FI-00100 HELSINKI
Tel.: +358 (0)9 121 4430
Fax: +358 (0)9 121 4242
E-mail: akatilaus@akateeminen.com
http://www.akateeminen.com

FRANCE
Please contact directly /
Merci de contacter directement
Council of Europe Publishing
Editions du Conseil de l'Europe
FR-67075 STRASBOURG cedex
Tel.: +33 (0)3 88 41 25 81
Fax: +33 (0)3 88 41 39 10
E-mail: publishing@coe.int
http://book.coe.int

Librairie Kléber
1 rue des Francs-Bourgeois
FR-67000 STRASBOURG
Tel.: +33 (0)3 88 15 78 88
Fax: +33 (0)3 88 15 78 80
E-mail: librairie-kleber@coe.int
http://www.librairie-kleber.com

**GERMANY/ALLEMAGNE
AUSTRIA/AUTRICHE**
W. Bertelsmann Verlag Gmbh @ Co KG
Auf dem Esch 4
D-33619 BIELEFELD
Tel.: +49 521 91101 13
Fax: +49 521 91101 19
E-mail: uno-verlag@wbv.de
www.uno-verlag.de

GREECE/GRÈCE
Librairie Kauffmann s.a.
Stadiou 28
GR-105 64 ATHINAI
Tel.: +30 210 32 55 321
Fax.: +30 210 32 30 320
E-mail: ord@otenet.gr
http://www.kauffmann.gr

HUNGARY/HONGRIE
Euro Info Service
Pannónia u. 58.
PF. 1039
HU-1136 BUDAPEST
Tel.: +36 1 329 2170
Fax: +36 1 349 2053
E-mail: euroinfo@euroinfo.hu
http://www.euroinfo.hu

ITALY/ITALIE
Licosa SpA
Via Duca di Calabria, 1/1
IT-50125 FIRENZE
Tel.: +39 0556 483215
Fax: +39 0556 41257
E-mail: licosa@licosa.com
http://www.licosa.com

NORWAY/NORVÈGE
Akademika
Postboks 84 Blindern
NO-0314 OSLO
Tel.: +47 2 218 8100
Fax: +47 2 218 8103
E-mail: support@akademika.no
http://www.akademika.no

POLAND/POLOGNE
Ars Polona JSC
25 Obroncow Street
PL-03-933 WARSZAWA
Tel.: +48 (0)22 509 86 00
Fax: +48 (0)22 509 86 10
E-mail: arspolona@arspolona.com.pl
http://www.arspolona.com.pl

PORTUGAL
Marka Lda
Rua dos Correeiros 61-3
PT-1100-162 LISBOA
Tel: 351 21 3224040
Fax: 351 21 3224044
Web: www.marka.pt
E mail: apoio.clientes@marka.pt

**RUSSIAN FEDERATION/
FÉDÉRATION DE RUSSIE**
Ves Mir
17b, Butlerova ul. - Office 338
RU-117342 MOSCOW
Tel.: +7 495 739 0971
Fax: +7 495 739 0971
E-mail: orders@vesmirbooks.ru
http://www.vesmirbooks.ru

SWITZERLAND/SUISSE
Planetis Sàrl
16 chemin des Pins
CH-1273 ARZIER
Tel.: +41 22 366 51 77
Fax: +41 22 366 51 78
E-mail: info@planetis.ch

UNITED KINGDOM/ROYAUME-UNI
The Stationery Office Ltd
PO Box 29
GB-NORWICH NR3 1GN
Tel.: +44 (0)870 600 5522
Fax: +44 (0)870 600 5533
E-mail: book.enquiries@tso.co.uk
http://www.tsoshop.co.uk

**UNITED STATES and CANADA/
ÉTATS-UNIS et CANADA**
Manhattan Publishing Co
670 White Plains Road
USA-10583 SCARSDALE, NY
Tel: +1 914 472 4500
Fax: +1 914 472 4316
E-mail: coe@manhattanpublishing.com
http://www.manhattanpublishing.com

Council of Europe Publishing/Editions du Conseil de l'Europe
FR-67075 STRASBOURG Cedex
Tel.: +33 (0)3 88 41 25 81 – Fax: +33 (0)3 88 41 39 10 – E-mail: publishing@coe.int – Website: http://book.coe.int